Also by Rohit Juneja

Loving Soulfully

God, You Sexy Devil

Exposing The Greatest Lie Ever Told

by

Rohit Juneja

God, You Sexy Devil

Exposing The Greatest Lie Ever Told

by Rohit Juneja

First Published October 2015

Copyright © by Rohit Juneja,

US Library of Congress

ISBN number: 978-0-9883989-3-1

(1) Religion > Spirituality (2) Body, Mind Spirit > Inspiration & Personal Growth

Contents

Acknowledgements... ix
Dedication xi
Introduction.. xiii
My Journey xvii
Journal xxiii

Messages From An Inner Voice.. 1
Chapter 1: I Am and I Am Not 3
Chapter 2: God - The Greatest Lie Ever Told............................. 11
Chapter 3: Fanatical Religion, The Root Cause Of Evil 21
Chapter 4: The Ultimate Contradiction 27
Chapter 5: The God Virus: As Above So Below 31
Chapter 6: God Does Not Believe in God 43
Chapter 7: Call Me With Love 51
Chapter 8: Listen to Your Soul 57
Chapter 9: Believe Nothing I Say 63

The Personhood of a Loving God... 69
Chapter 10: The Soul's Heroic Journey...................................... 71
Chapter 11: Understanding God 77
Chapter 12: Creating a Better God... 81
Chapter 13: Who or What is God?... 87
Chapter 14: The Impersonal Energy of God.............................. 93

Chapter 15: Individuated Oneness 99
Chapter 16: I Am All 105
Chapter 17: The Personhood of God 111
Chapter 18: An Exquisitely Sexy God 119
Chapter 19: The Love Trinity 123

What The Hell is Going On? 129
Chapter 20: You Are Burning in Hell Right Now 131
Chapter 21: Dark Energy Vibrational Illusion (d.e.v.il) 139
Chapter 22: God and the Devil are One 147
Chapter 23: No More Blame, Fairness and Justice 153
Chapter 24: Judging God to Hell 161
Chapter 25: Using God 167
Chapter 26: The Futility of Prayer, Rituals and Worship 173

The Age of The Messiahs 177
Chapter 27: Saving Humanity From Itself 179
Chapter 28: The Neo-Messiahs of Politics, Science and
         Technology 189
Chapter 29: Alien Demigods 197
Chapter 30: The Seven Deadly Flaws of Salvation 207
Chapter 31: The Curse of Righteousness 225
Chapter 32: The Rise and Fall of Fanaticism 235
Chapter 33: Religion, the Antithesis of God 241
Chapter 34: The Way Out 245

The Age of Awakening 251
Chapter 35: The Human Dinosaur 253
Chapter 36: The Illusion of Virtual Sensory Reality 257
Chapter 37: The Ever Changing Word of God 263
Chapter 38: The Path of the Mystics 269
Chapter 39: Communion With God 275
Chapter 40: Thousands of Christs, Krishnas & Buddhas 285
Chapter 41: Eclectic Wisdom 293
Chapter 42: Loving God Fearlessly 297
Chapter 43: Save Yourself Soulfully 301

About the Author 305

Acknowledgements

I am deeply grateful and indebted to the following people:

My wonderful parents, Promila and Prakash, as well as my precious daughter Govindi for unconditionally loving me and steadfastly standing by my side through all the ups and downs of my life.

My dear Anu, Elisa, Noopur, Kainat and Ayesha for all your love, for passionately believing in me and motivating me.

All my wonderful friends in San Diego, Los Angeles, India and around the world, especially Sumit, Clarity, Zhanna, Astha, Cathy and Lina, for your love, support and being such an important part of my life.

A special thanks to Meshell and Nathalie for your invaluable feedback and comments.

Winnie, with whose inspiration I began to turn within and connect with my inner voice.

Asudharam, whose awe inspiring love for God deeply touched my heart and soul.

JSR Madhukar my soul brother for always bringing me closer to God.

Sarah McNamara and Cheelu Chandaran, for your meticulous and inspired editing work. Working with you has been a memorable experience.

Paloma Gauthier at Natural Records Studio for designing the wonderful book cover.

Thank you dear reader for being part of this incredible journey. May this book inspire you to form a loving relationship with God. This book is the greatest miracle I have experienced. I share it with you in the hope that it will bring to you the gifts of inspiration, clarity and wisdom that it gave me. I believe that if you remain open, these words will grow like a seed within you, helping you to evolve, experience the magic of your soul and develop a deeply loving and intimate relationship with God. In time our souls will connect, uniting us in an ever expanding circle of love that will transform our world

I dedicate this book to Bankebihari and Asudharam
For inspiring me to write, to surrender and fearlessly love God.

Dear Beloved, God, thank you for unconditionally loving me, guiding me and being with me every step of this long and exciting journey. My gifts, abilities, everything that I am and all that I have written has come from you. I humbly offer myself and this book to you with deepest gratitude. If I have unintentionally added or distorted anything, please forgive me. May your words reach all those whom you intended them for.

Introduction

I use the word God because this is how most people refer to the Source of all that is. You may prefer to replace this word with Goddess, Universe, Source, Energy, Light, Christ, Buddha, Allah, Krishna, Rama or any other name that you choose to ascribe to a Higher Power. Shakespeare once wrote, "a rose by any other name would smell as sweet" and so it is with God. In this book, as far as possible, I will use the terms God, God of Love, Loving God, Source or inner voice whenever I refer to the One that speaks to me. I will use the phrase 'God of religion' when I refer to the distorted notion of God that religion invented.

Since the beginning of time human beings have wondered, speculated and theorized about the nature of the Universe, its Creator and the purpose of their existence. Humankind has explored a vast array of beliefs, such as nature worship, pantheism, polytheism, paganism and monotheism. Perhaps the most powerful influence on humanity came from the three most prominent monotheistic religions: Judaism, Christianity and Islam. They presented humanity with sons, messiahs, messengers, prophets and saviors who they claimed were representatives of God and had come to save the world. Armed with heaven as the carrot and hell as the stick, they lured us into believing their sacred scriptures. They shaped our social norms, families, judiciary, politics and almost every aspect of our world with their religious doctrine. They inspired us to conquer, capture and indoctrinate people all over the world with their version of the truth.

Our adventure into monotheism has had startling consequences that opened the floodgates for hitherto unimaginable destruction and death. Millions of people have been killed in the name of religion, perhaps more than all humans killed by war, genocide, dictators, murder and crime over the ages. At the same time, the psychologically devastating power of shame, guilt, hate, fear, judgment and repression, brought about as a direct or indirect consequence of religious theology, has violated almost every human being that has lived on this planet over thousands of years. To add insult to injury, they informed us that God is waiting for "judgment day" to send billions of us, his children, who didn't accept the messiah, to suffer eternally in hell!

Why did our natural curiosity and search for meaning turn into such a destructive force? Why did we become so blind and brainwashed? Why was the absurdity of these religious teachings not obvious to most of us? Why did we choose fear over love, suffering over pleasure and dogma over freedom?

I had so many questions.

Instead of rejecting God, I chose to turn to him for answers. If he could speak with the messiahs, messengers, apostles and prophets, then he would certainly speak with me. It seemed like a perfectly good idea, although I can now see how absurd or even arrogant it might seem to some followers of religion. Imagine, if Christ, Mohammed or Buddha had worried about what people might think they, too, would never have dared to reach out and listen to God. In my naiveté I turned to God, trusting that he/she would talk to me.

I learnt to silence my mind, then I asked questions and waited patiently for a reply. An inner voice responded by asking me to write. I was astonished by what emerged. Its message was unlike anything I had ever come across.

It said that it was the voice of God, that religion was the greatest lie ever told and that the God of religion was a man made myth. It declared that God, the Source of all existence is a loving consciousness, a non-physical being, an undefinable, eternal field of infinite possibilities that is constantly growing, evolving and reinventing itself.

Through this conversation I learnt that God experiences her/him self through each of us. As we experience the dualities of our lives such as love and hate, pleasure and pain: as we transform and evolve, God does too.

I learnt that God does not relate to our distorted notions of right and wrong, good and evil heaven and hell. These judgmental, conditional, dualistic ideals are mentally concocted creations that mean nothing to God. I discovered that God is not moral, good holy or righteous. God neither wrote any scriptures, nor gave any commandments, nor will s/he ever judge anyone. We were created with free will, to desire, manifest and do whatever we want. God would never punish, judge or stand in our way, no matter what we do. At the same time, God's intention is to connect with each of us individually, love us unconditionally and gently guide us from within. There is no pressure to listen to God or obey his will.

I understood that the purpose of coming into this world was not so that we could quickly get out of it and go to heaven or the Light. We came to discover the magnificence of who we are, love ourselves and discover the manifold truths about God.

I do not ask you to believe me or the inner voice that speaks to me. I only urge you read the message of love contained within these pages and consider the possibilities it has put forth. Please listen to your own inner voice before believing anything I write or arriving at any conclusion.

In the past century, it seems as if Source or God has been actively communicating with thousands of people all over the world. Perhaps this is the beginning of some form of divine intervention that is being downloaded to and through many of us. The plan seems to be designed to change our consciousness through an expansion of wisdom and insight that will counter the modern day escalation of religious fanaticism. As the chaos and destruction in the world have increased, at the same time the opportunities to rapidly accelerate our soul's evolutionary journey through this physical world have multiplied exponentially. As the negative has grown, so too has the positive. The time has come, when divine wisdom and its actualization are no longer the exclusive domain of messiahs and gurus, but rather something that each of us can easily access and effortlessly integrate into our lives without complex and arduous processes.

We live in extraordinary times!

My Journey

As a teenager I was an agnostic with lots of questions. At thirteen I remember thinking that until I found answers to my questions, I did not want to choose a career or waste my time on trivial pursuits such as accumulating money, getting married or having children. Life didn't make sense to me. It seemed like a movie with a pathetic ending. I would often wonder, "what is the use of working hard and doing so many things if the ultimate conclusion is that we will die and leave it all behind? What is the purpose of life? What is the point of existence? Why is there so much suffering in the world? If there is a God, where is s/he, why isn't s/he helping us and what does he want from us?

I refused to blindly believe anything. I read everything I could get my hands on; ancient scriptures, modern self-help books, psychology, philosophy and science. I discussed, argued and listened to anyone who had a theory, anyone who was willing to try and answer my questions. I was relentless in my search. I met and followed gurus and tried various spiritual practices but none of the teachings seemed to truly satisfy me. Each time I thought I had the answer, it ultimately turned out to be inadequate and ineffective. The search for truth, meaning and purpose seemed to become an endless pursuit.

Over the years I went from agnostic to religious fanatic to freethinker. I also wore many professional hats: dishwasher, monk, salesman, art dealer, entrepreneur, innovator, counselor, healer and therapist. Each time I thought I had the answer, as if by perfect design, my seemingly impregnable fortresses of truth came tumbling down. The distortions and fallacies on my path would become exposed, shaking me out of complacency, leaving me feeling very foolish and empty. Yet each time I reached a dead end another door opened. The night gradually turned to day as the rays of new insight began to trickle through. In hindsight, I can see that it has been a grand adventure, unfolding at its own pace, revealing its mysteries, filling me with wonder and excitement with each new discovery.

For ten years I tried various forms of meditation but failed miserably. Instead of stopping, my thoughts would race faster than ever. The incessant flow of mental chatter made me feel heavy and drained. Eventually I gave up. One day, while driving down the highway, listening to music, something strange happened: my thoughts abruptly stopped. I was not meditating or doing anything yet my mind had become completely still. For the first time, I experienced a calm, peaceful, joyful and expansive feeling that seemed to envelop me in its warm embrace. I was fully present to the here and now. I was looking, hearing and experiencing everything around me with an inexplicable sense of clarity and awareness. At the same time it seemed as though I had stepped into another world. All problems and imperfections seemed to disappear and in their place was a wonderful feeling that everything in life was intrinsically good and that nothing could ever harm me. Everything appeared beautiful. It was like being in love. I felt happy, light headed and peaceful for no reason at all. I had done nothing to enter this "zone." It had happened effortlessly.

In the days following this experience I kept wondering if it was really so simple and natural to reach this state of "no-mind." Had I had been trying too hard all these years? The experience I had had was addictive and I longed to keep going back to it. I gradually began to discover that all I had to do was pause, take a deep breath and be present to my breathing. I would easily and effortlessly enter this blissful state of mind and stay there for as long as I liked. In time it became my natural state, my inner home, the foundation from where I began to experience my life. A deep inner shift had occurred. It germinated, grew and expanded. I started experiencing things I had heard and read about from spiritual teachers and authors. I found that I could talk back to my mind and redirect it with compassion. Life no longer felt like a struggle. Tension, anxiety and concern about survival vanished. No matter what happened externally, within myself I felt abundant, free and fearless. The spiritual dimension was now a tangible reality that was readily available whenever I wanted to tune into it.

With a little help and encouragement from friends and guides, I learnt to go deeper into this stillness, ask questions and listen to my inner voice. When I first began to hear it, I didn't trust what it was telling me. I had been addicted to blindly believing my mentally concocted thoughts. It was hard to step back and observe the subtle differences between the voices of mind and spirit. The inner voice was not pushy, critical, loud or demanding like my mind. It was a gentle, soulful whisper that was lucid, insightful and filled with wisdom. It seemed to have answers to my questions. Instead of the heaviness that accompanied thinking, this inner voice made me feel light, inspired, uplifted and clear headed whenever I listened to it. It guided me patiently through various life situations and I began to develop trust.

I grew up in a Hindu family. Concepts like heaven, hell, judgment and sin, repentance and evil were not part of my upbringing. I was taught that God had many avatars or incarnations. Out of all the forms of God, the one that has most appealed to me, since childhood, was Krishna. He was loving, beautiful, youthful, playful and absolutely adorable. One day, while visiting a temple in Vrindavan, India, my dear spiritual guide Asudharam invited me to ask the deity Bankebihari, a form of Krishna, any question I might have. "He will answer all your questions," Asudharam reassured me. Understandably, my first thought was one of utter disbelief. I had visited innumerable temples and places of worship and saw deities simply standing on their altar as stone idols while people worshipped them. Suspending all doubts and past experiences, I decided to give it a try and began speaking with Bankebihari. I paused to listen. I suddenly became aware of a voice inside my head, talking to me, answering all my questions. The responses were as clear as if someone was standing right next to me and speaking into my mind. I listened in a trance-like state and felt the words enter deep into my subconscious. I felt light, peaceful and safe. There were hundreds of people around me, chanting, praying, talking and moving around but I found myself undisturbed by the hustle and bustle. In that moment, nothing seemed to exist except this inner voice and the conversation we were having. We talked for an hour, about my life, my dreams and the direction in which I should proceed. The words were encouraging, hopeful and loving. When I stepped out of the temple I had very little recollection of what we had spoken about. Over the next two years I kept visiting every month, eagerly looking forward to these wonderful chats.

Then one day Bankebihari, changed his tune. He insisted that I write down our conversations. He said, "You forget everything we talk about when you leave the temple. Besides, there is so much more I want to tell you." I laughed. The guidance I was receiving was personal, why would anyone be interested in reading about my problems? Besides, the temple was extremely crowded and noisy, I could barely stand, how would I possibly write? I chose to ignore his request and he refused to speak with me any further till I did. We were at a stalemate. Six months had gone by and one day, out of the blue, a friend handed me a copy of "Conversations with God, Part 1" by Neale Donald Walsh. As I read I began to wonder, "did he want me to write a book and communicate something important?" I felt a surge of excitement welling up inside me. I had to find out. I agreed to write on the condition that he would come to me wherever I was and he agreed. I decided to open my heart and mind, to trust and receive, to avoid any preconceived notions, biases and beliefs. I asked questions and he began dictating his amazing message with clarity and simplicity.

As I wrote, the words began to flow effortlessly, page after page, thought after incredible thought. The writing had lucidity and a style that was definitely not mine. It tapped into things I had heard, read or experienced. Yet its message was unlike anything I had ever come across.

There was no plan, draft, outline or concept. I had no clue what the next word or sentence might be or even if it would make any sense. I felt as if I was walking blindfolded, letting the river of words carry me into uncharted territory. The unknown beckoned, the unexpected was happening. It was as if time had stopped and I was witnessing the miracle that was taking birth through me. At first I was unsure of where all this was heading but it soon became clear that I was being used to communicate a vital message.

This book went through many layers of recreating itself. From the time I first began writing until the time it was finished, fifteen years had passed. During this time, the messages that I had received made me confront my deepest fears and find my deepest truth. They transformed my personality, my energy and my entire being. I felt as if I was being sculpted, empowered and recreated from the inside out. The more I let go of my deeply held subconscious fears of being persecuted and ridiculed for writing these words, the clearer, more powerful and fearless the messages became. The process of writing turned out to be a deeply healing, uplifting and co-creative process.

I am deeply grateful and humbled by the transformative gifts this book has given me. I share my experience in the hope that perhaps you, dear reader, may see yourself in my search and be inspired to listen to your own inner voice. May you receive the guidance you need along with the answers to your own questions.

Journal

Each chapter of the hard copy book has either one or two blank pages after it. This is to allow you to reflect on what you have read, make notes and journal your insights.

At any time you, if you feel like sharing your thoughts and opinions with the author and the larger community of readers, we would love to hear your feedback, questions, likes and dislikes at GodYouSexyDevil.wordpress.com

Your reviews would be much appreciated on amazon.com, Apple iBooks and Goodreads.

Thank you for joining us in creating a loving God for a better world.

Messages From An Inner Voice

CHAPTER 1

I Am and I Am Not

Rohit: Despite religion, science and technology, this wonderful world is in a terrible mess. War, famine, poverty, disease, fanaticism, abuse, greed, environmental destruction and suffering are rampant and constantly increasing. The madness keeps escalating with each passing year, threatening to destroy this planet. I call on you God, Source of all that is, to guide me and show me the way. I have tried everything, but nothing in this world makes sense to me. I know you are there. I trust you, I open my heart, mind and soul to you. Please speak to me. I am ready to listen.

Inner Voice: I Am here. I have been with you always. I have been longing to speak with you but are you willing to hear the truth, the whole truth and nothing but the truth? I want to be known as I am and for you to know yourself as you are. I want to support humanity and resolve the conflict, struggle, suffering and chaos in your world. Unfortunately, to accomplish this is not easy because you have all been brainwashed, programmed and conditioned to believe in untruths. When the majority of people believe a lie, it becomes the truth and the truth becomes a lie. Anyone who dares expose the lie is likely to be called foolish or even crazy. Over the centuries such people were called heretics, infidels and traitors. They were burned at the stake, crucified, tortured and mercilessly killed. Your world appears to have changed externally but the fanaticism of those who think they know the truth has taken new forms and has grown to epic proportions. The forces that have been unleashed now threaten to destroy the planet and its inhabitants. Despite the enormous wealth of knowledge that you all share through technology, the core truths about life, self and God, continue to remain elusive. What I wish to say is neither pleasant nor comfortable. It will contradict much of what you have heard, believed or held sacred. If you share my words with others you are likely to be judged, criticized, ridiculed or even persecuted. Are you sure you still want to talk with me?

Rohit: My mind seems still, there are no thoughts except a gentle whisper responding to my question. Is this the voice of my mind, my soul, an alien entity or someone else? Who are you? Are you God? Please identify yourself. I am ready to listen to your version of the truth. I am not afraid of the consequences.

Inner Voice: I speak through you, as a voice in your head, using your intellect, tapping into your experience and aligning with your consciousness, but only to the extent that you are open, empty and receptive, can I reveal myself. My attempt is to breakthrough your limitations, expand your imagination, open your body, mind, heart and soul. Then perhaps you will be able to glimpse some part of me and get a sense of who I am.

I am God and I am not. I am God but not the God you believe in. I am the one you seek but not the one you know. If you are attached to what you know from religion, scriptures, priests, gurus and science then all that I am about to say will mean nothing to you. Your belief in the known will not allow you to discover the unknown. I invite you to put aside your knowing and experience the mystery, the magic, the miracle and the true nature of God that has been hidden from your world for thousands of years. The time has come for the truth to be revealed.

The truth is, I Am ... the One and only God. I Am ... the God of every religion that ever existed. I Am ... the Light, the Universe, the Source, the Creator of everything and everyone. I Am ... the origin and the essence of all that is material and spiritual, I Am ... the cause and the effect, the creation and the dissolution, the origin and the destination of all that is. I Am ... the all in One and the One in all, which means that I am in everything and everyone and yet I exist separate from my creation as a unique, individuated, being. I Am ... past, present and future, existence and non-existence, everything and nothing, everywhere and nowhere. I Am ... God and the devil, good and evil, light and darkness. I Am ... every object, creature, thought, creation, idea or action that anyone ever had, did or will do. Above all, I Am ... love, unconditional, limitless, eternal and pure love.

I am in every scripture, place of worship and spiritual path. I am the son of God, the messenger of God and the guru - all in One. I am in everyone. Every theist and atheist, saint and sinner, messiah and murderer, priest and prisoner is an expression of my endless kaleidoscopic diversity.

I am everywhere. Every bar and temple, whorehouse and church, prison and mosque, mansion and hutment is my home.

I cannot be limited to any singular name, form or theology. All names for God, since time immemorial, have been attempts to describe the indescribable. I am Jesus, Yahweh, Elohim, Allah, Nanak, Buddha, Rama and Krishna. I am simultaneously all of them and yet each one of you has been led to believe that your God is the only God and that all the others are impostors or devils. The real devils are in fact the short sighted, immature, unrealized preachers who, through their warped, arrogant, fear-filled teachings, have brought about the greatest wedge between humanity.

I want to be very clear from the beginning that my words are not directed at highly evolved beings such as Christ, Moses, Mohammed, Buddha, Nanak etc. or the kind hearted, open minded, liberal believers who have understood the deeper intent of their message. Whenever I use the words religion, scriptures, messiahs, saviors or messengers, I am referring to the distorted interpretations propagated by the conservative, orthodox, fanatics and fundamentalists of all religions. These devils in pious garb have divided the planet into religious sects, communities, and countries,wreaking havoc on Earth. In their ignorance they have brought humanity to the brink of chaos and destruction. Their influence must be stopped before it spreads any further.

Rohit: Why do have me write I Am ...?

God: I Am... means that I am infinite and inconceivable. You can add anything after I Am ... and it will be true. I am all of everything. I am all that is good and bad, divine and sinful, painful and pleasurable, dark and light. I am all theories, philosophies and doctrines. All that you perceive, know, think, imagine, postulate, experience and create comes from me. Words cannot comprehend me, definitions cannot limit me, beliefs cannot bind me. I am infinitely expanding, evolving and reinventing myself. Any notion you have of me is outdated the moment you think of it. Whatever you believe about me can only be partially true, an aspect of truth or a possibility.

Whatever you think or believe about me is very likely to be limited, flawed and untrue. For example, if you believe that I am good, fair, wise, honest or truthful then you have deceived yourself. I am all of this, its opposite too, and far more than you can imagine. I exist in a state of consciousness where definition is meaningless, duality is non existent, opposites are redundant, comparisons are pointless and measurements are worthless. Good is no better than bad, right is no better than wrong, peace is no better than war, justice is no better than injustice.

I am what I am, regardless of what anyone thinks, believes or says. Experience me as I am, know me as I am and love me as I am.

I Am … also refers to the union of the two aspects of spiritual reality, the simultaneous existence of separateness (I) and Oneness (Am), the inconceivable co-existence of the individuated being, God and the all pervading energy of God.

I am the one you have been looking for in all of your endeavors, in all of your desires and in all of those whom you love. I am the one who accepts you as you are. I am the one who loves you regardless of what you do. I am the one who sees how beautiful, powerful and magnificent you are. I am the one who believes in you, always.

I am you and you are me. We are the same energy, essence and spirit. Yet, we are all different, unique, individuated and special. We are all simultaneously and inconceivably One and different! All humans are Gods and God is as human as you are.

Journal

CHAPTER 2

God - The Greatest Lie Ever Told

God: They call me God. I'm supposed to be that strange dude who lives in the sky in some bizarre and boring place called heaven. Some believe that I am nameless and formless while others believe that I am an old man, with a long beard and white robes, surrounded by harp-playing, angels. Holy baloney!! Welcome to the land of religious mythology, where faith turns intelligent, caring people into mindless, hateful robots; where fanatical devils masquerade as priests, preaching their distorted interpretations of the word of God. Religious pimps have been prostituting me for thousands of years, raping your minds with their lies and deception, spreading hate and fanaticism throughout the world.

Rohit: You seem really upset!

God: Did you expect me to peaceful and emotionless? I am not one dimensional, either all love and peace or all judgment and anger. I am as human as you are and you are as divine as I am. I feel as you do but I am not defined by my feelings, I feel anger but I am not a "wrathful" angry person. I vibrate at the highest frequency in the Universe - love, but this love is not sterile and pure, it is in fact colorful and rich with emotion and passion. I plead with you to take me off from the pedestal of perfection, the holy altar of divinity and allow me to be real with you. I want to share my feelings with you, be vulnerable and reveal all of myself. A real relationship cannot be based on idealization, it must be based on honesty, truth and acceptance of who we are. Many of you have called on me and vented your feelings of frustration, anger, hurt and sadness. Now I am asking you to do the same for me. Please hold space for me as you would for your loved ones when they need someone to hear them and express what is in their heart. After a long time I have found in you, someone who is willing to hear me, accept me and love me as I am, one who will not limit me to the cage of their preconceived notions. Allow me to vent what is in my heart and trust that, behind everything I say, is the sincere intention for all of us to deepen in love and create a better world.

I have been quiet a long time and its high time for me to do some P.R. to clear up my reputation and get an image makeover. That's a hard feat to accomplish when people already have you pegged, slotted and labeled; when so called sacred scriptures declare you to be that which you are not; when priests stand on lofty pulpits threatening fire and brimstone to brainwashed believers; when atheists, who see through the lies, choose to walk away from the mess and have nothing to do with it.

I am not planning on being politically correct or polite. It's time to call a spade a spade and end the madness that has killed millions of people in the name of God. The time has come to be remove all ambiguity and clearly reveal the truth about God so we may work together to bring peace, love and happiness back to Earth.

In the words of Nietzsche, "God is dead!" In fact the God that most of you believe in (or disbelieve) never existed. Don't get me wrong. God exists! In fact, only God exists and nothing exists that is not God.

God is the greatest lie ever told, religion is the ultimate conspiracy and the scriptures the most powerful medium of mass brainwashing ever invented by man. For the most part, the scriptures that people believe in and the God they worship are a giant hoax. It is a lie ensconced in beautiful verse, poetic language, brilliant scholarship and erudition. It is a myth that has been perpetuated for thousands of years and upheld by the most trusted, revered and respected religious authorities. It is an untruth that has been accepted as the truth by millions of devout followers who blindly believe that their particular God, messiah and scripture are the absolute truth and the only way to get to heaven.

Those who did not believe the lie and opposed it were considered sinners, heretics, blasphemers and infidels. They were tortured, burnt, raped, looted and murdered for daring to expose the lie. Based on these lies, man went to war, ruled societies, judged criminals, controlled women, punished children and discriminated against all those who were of a different race, caste, color, gender, religion or nationality. From this grand deception came the greatest violence in the history of humankind.

Adolf Hitler said, "in the big lie there is always a certain force of credibility. The great mass of people will more easily fall victim to a big lie than to a small one." For a lie to be believable it must be a big lie and it must be based on some measure of truth. A complete lie would never have gone undetected for this long. A conspiracy to effectively brainwash millions of people must touch their deepest fears and longings, leaving them with no other choice but to surrender their free will, without considering the consequences. It was this skillful blending of truth and untruth, fact and fiction, which led to the creation of man's ultimate masterpiece – God!

The scriptures, no doubt are filled with great truths and words of wisdom, but even a slight distortion of truth is enough to make monsters out of angels and devils out of saints. The greater the light of truth, the darker the shadow born from its corruption and the more damaging its impact on the minds of sincere, innocent seekers. When an honest person speaks a lie it is assumed to be the truth and when a dishonest person speaks a truth he is still not believed. When the so-called upholders of morality, values and piety speak an untruth based on the ultimate authority of God, then no matter how bizarre the lie, it will be believed and obeyed blindly.

The mythical web of beliefs woven by religious fanatics runs so contrary to common sense, yet millions of intelligent, decent people have been brainwashed to accept these absurd concoctions as gospel truth. They would have you believe that my job is to judge people, to let the good ones come to heaven and send the bad ones to hell. They say that if you, my children, do not obey me then I will condemn you to burn eternally in hell! Religious fear-mongers insist that you must fear God and love God too, for to fear God is to love God! (How can you possibly love someone whom you fear?) They claim that not even a blade of grass moves without my will but if you do something against my will then you will be held accountable and punished! (If I am the one who does everything then shouldn't I be going to hell?) They preach that I created you and gave you free will but if you don't follow my commandments I will destroy you forever! (Doesn't free will mean that you are free to do whatever you will?) If you must follow commandments then either free will is a myth or the commandments are a lie.) They say that God is great and you are all insignificant, that God must be worshiped and obeyed or the wrath of God will fall upon you. They claim that God is judgmental, angry, vindictive, puritanical, jealous and autocratic. At the same time he is also supposed to be loving, merciful, forgiving and compassionate: sounds like someone with a mood disorder, possibly schizophrenic, definitely in desperate need of anger management classes. These are just but a few of the illogical and contradictory ways in which they have portrayed me.

Rohit: Some religious people argue that we are given free will to either accept or reject God. If we reject him, we are choosing, with our free will, to go to hell. It's not God punishing us per se, but rather us denying him and his gift of salvation. I looked up the dictionary meaning of free will and it says, "the power of acting without the constraint of necessity or fate; the ability to act at one's own discretion."

God: There is only one supreme law or commandment in the Universe: free will. You have all been given unconditional freedom to do as you will and fulfill all your desires. At the same time I built in to the Universe a karmic system of checks and balances. Whenever you act against the free will of another living being or even the planet, then your transgression will be mirrored back to you as consequences. This universal principle of cause and effect, action and reaction, has nothing to do with any faith or belief system.

Rohit: This was stated in the Bible as, "do to others as you would have them do to you."

God: This is a universal principle. As for rejecting God, that is why this physical Universe was created, so that you may have the freedom to discover your essence or live in illusion, to love or hate each other, to choose or reject God. In this world you may experience the contrast between a life without God or a life in communion with God. You may reject the God of religion but I am not the property of any institution. How will reject that which is everywhere you go, in everyone that you love and everything that you desire. I am in the air, the water, the food, the sunshine, in every cell of your body. To truly reject God you must turn away from life which some have achieved by becoming addicted to their mind or a substance that controls their mind. The mind is the doorway to heaven or hell. Mental Addiction takes many forms such as incessant thinking, narcissism, depression, insanity etc. The hellish state of mind that many of you experience is very likely due to your disconnection with God. Those who silence their minds find heaven on Earth and experience God everywhere.

Most religions say more or less the same thing. It's as if they have plagiarized each others ideas, put their own spin on it and voila! They have repackaged the same old mythology and created their unique brand of God. Their arrogant priests proudly proclaim that their way is the only way that only you can get to heaven and all non-believers are heretics or infidels. If you must con the world you might as well get together and come up with a more plausible story. That way you don't spoil the market. Religious leaders should have converged and arrived at a consensus around creation, God, hell, heaven etc. You can't simultaneously have a variety of Gods, each claiming to be the only one, creating the same Universe and taking the credit for it. You can't have each one saying their messiah or prophet is the only way. You can't have a hell and no hell, a devil and no devil. All these stories can't be true. Someone's story has to be false. Who will decide? Whose God will be the real God? Whose messiah will be the real savior? Whose story of creation will be considered authentic? Will it be the God of the majority, the God of the richest, the God of those with the most powerful weapons or the ones who kill the most people?

They all say that the other's God is false. I agree. They are all correct. The reality is that they are all worshiping false Gods, distorted scriptures and evil preachers. What shall we do? Should we get rid of them all, shred all their scriptures, bomb all their places of worship, burn all the priests at the stake or stone them to death, the way they killed millions of innocent people throughout the ages? Certainly not! It is true that they are deluded, fanatical, propagators of falsehood. They are guilty of having hidden the truth about God and are blind to the hell on Earth that their lies have created. But they cannot be blamed. If there were no believers they would have been out of business a long time ago. Everyone is responsible for this chaos. It is the human mind's affinity for instant gratification, wishful thinking and quick fixes that has seduced billions of devout followers. It is natural for the mind to want a savior, someone who will solve all the problems, fulfill all desires, end all miseries and take you to a better place. Most people do not want to work on improving themselves, taking responsibility for their actions and shaping their own reality. That's just too much work! Its so much easier to have someone die for them, wave a magic wand and fix everything.

Journal

CHAPTER 3

Fanatical Religion, The Root Cause Of Evil

Rohit: Are your words, in this book or any other, the absolute truth, the law for humanity or the ultimate word of God?

God: People who call their scripture "the word of God" are often more interested in the word "the" rather than in understanding God. The word "the" to them usually signifies that their book is the one and only, the most exclusive and perfect, the ultimate and final word of God. There is a deep rooted arrogance in this declaration, a rejection of all past writings inspired by God and a muzzle placed on God so that he may never speak again to anyone. They are afraid that God may contradict their theology, disrupt their institutions and confuse their cult of mindless fanaticism.

This book is certainly the word of God. As were the original writings of every scripture, millions of scientific theories and inventions, works of art, music, poetry and literature all over the world. They were inspired by me but none of them are perfect, unchanging or absolute. The word of

God is not finite, static or frozen in time, it is in fact infinite, unlimited and constantly evolving. God is perpetually expanding and changing, as are you and everything in the Universe. If things didn't keep changing life would be boring, if we didn't keep learning we would stagnate, if we didn't endlessly evolve we would become extinct. There is no perfection, no end point and no finality in the Universe. Everything is constantly in flux and nothing is ever the same. All knowledge is forever incomplete, all achievement meaningless and all that exists ultimately disintegrates and dies. Thats just the way the Universe was designed. Embrace these simple truths and you will thrive, resist them and you may wither and become extinct.

The only people who don't seem to understand this are everyone because the human mind won't let you. It wants to believe in a heaven that is forever, a God who is perfect and a scripture that is absolute, infallible and flawless in every way. The same lack of objectivity often shows up in science, technology or medicine, it shows up in the way you think about relationships, aging and work because whichever way you spin the roulette wheel of the mind, it must land in the same place: fanaticism. The mind, by default, believes that whatever it thinks is true, what the community thinks is even more true and what God thinks is the unassailable truth. The disease of fanaticism is not unique to religion it is the core affliction of the mind. Only one who has tamed the mind will conquer this tendency and know the meaning of true power. To achieve this we must understand how fanaticism works and for this purpose we shall take a good look at the way it influenced every religion throughout the world.

Fundamentalist religions have been the greatest cause of war, destruction and unnatural death in the history of this planet. Their interpretation of scripture is a figment of human imagination, an abomination that has made a mockery of God. The concept of God that they preach is so full of holes that it doesn't stand up to examination, logic or common sense, not even for a moment. It does however have all the ingredients of an epic story, a fabulous drama or a blockbuster movie. For thousands of years it has inspired millions to hate, kill, torture and destroy each other in the name of God.

Rohit: It is reported that Hitler was responsible for the systematic killing of between six to twelve million Jews. Most of them were either shot or killed in gas chambers where they died in a matter of minutes. In contrast, God's fanatical armies have killed tens of millions of people in inquisitions, ethnic cleansing and holy wars. To add insult to injury, on "judgment day" the fanatics say that God will send all non believers to burn in the fires of hell for eternity. There are almost two billion Christians and close to that many Muslims on the planet at this time. So it stands to reason, depending on whose side you take, that the remaining, more than five billion non believers, God's own children, are to be sent to hell to burn for eternity. That would make God the greatest tyrant of all time.

God: Tyrants have been known to torture people for days or even years but no tyrant has ever existed with the power to torture someone forever. They may have tortured an enemy but rarely would they have harmed a loved one and certainly not their own children. Throughout history, folklore and mythology, never has there existed a depraved creature, more cruel, vicious and merciless than the God of religion. This demented God, if he ever existed, would have been the most evil being, the greatest devil, the most warped genocidal mass murderer or psychopath, conceivable. Having projected their worst fears on God, the concocters of religion declared that their God was loving, just and forgiving. By concepts such as "original sin," puritanical preachers damned humanity to everlasting guilt and shame. By virtue of their absurd standards of morality, virtue and goodness, they set the stage for psychologically traumatizing people into feeling undeserving, unworthy and unlovable. Many embraced their worthless, sinful status and immersed themselves in horrific crimes. The majority worked hard to prove themselves worthy by being good and pious, by conforming to the diktats of society, politics and religion or by seeking endless therapy to rid themselves of their eternal shame. Using these fear filled, manipulative ploys, many preachers demanded blind faith and fanaticism as the price for salvation.

In nature, all polarities generate an equal and opposite force in order to bring about balance and equilibrium. Religion focused its energies on making people good. The polar opposite of good is evil, just as the polarity of light is darkness. As the light of goodness grew stronger, it birthed unprecedented levels of darkness and evil. As the power and influence of religion expanded, so did the the power of evil. Good and evil fed on each other, hated each other and danced throughout planet Earth. In their wake they wrought havoc and chaos, fear and perversion, piety and corruption.

The tentacles of this pernicious evil force, disguised as religion, have spread themselves into every aspect of your lives. Government, judiciary, police, armed forces, business, science, art, music, literature, cinema, parenting, relationships - all carry elements of this bizarre phenomenon.

Almost every human mind has been polluted by the religiously created culture of shame, guilt, fear, judgment, superiority, greed, abuse, autocracy, vengeance, violence and war.

In its attempt to stamp out evil and establish goodness, religion unknowingly unleashed the greatest evil ever seen anywhere in the Universe. In its hatred for evil, religion became the root cause of evil!

That which you hate, you become!

Journal

CHAPTER 4

The Ultimate Contradiction

God: Most religions ask you to love God but have nothing lovable to tell you about God. How can you love someone you know nothing about? The God that they invented has nothing better to do than sit on a throne, spy on everything you do, invade your privacy and watch your every move. What a boring, dull character this God must be! He controls everything you do, tells you how to live your life, how to have sex, what to eat, how to pray, how to think, what to believe and how much money you should give to your religion. Like "big brother" he watches your every move, keeps a record of everything you do and judges all of your actions. That would make God the greatest dictator, the ultimate control-freak and sick pervert of all time! It's no wonder that they fear him instead of loving him, use him to save themselves from hell and bribe their way into heaven.

Religion taught that no one should approach God directly. Only the priests know the will of God. They are justified in their fear and wanting to keep you from God. I, the real God, am unpredictable, uncontrollable and unmanageable. That was why they restricted their followers to a straight and narrow path, a one-way communication with God through prayer, scripture, hymns and rituals. You could talk to God but God would not speak with you. Anyone who said he was listening to God would be declared a heretic and banished or persecuted. Their efforts to shut me up were extremely effective.

The primary focus of most religions was not on God because they knew very little about me. Instead, they have focused their energies on controlling your lifestyle, using heaven as the carrot and hell as the stick with which to subliminally beat you into submission. They told you how to how to behave and dress, what to think and feel, what you should and should not do. You were told that to appease God you must pray, sing and worship him; you must perform austerities, be good and do charity; above all you must obey, fear and love God.

May I ask why? Why would the Source of everything be impressed by your childish acts of piety, sacrifice and goodness? What sort of egomaniac would I be if wanted everyone to bow down to me and obey me out of fear? What sort of fiendish father would I be if I gave some of my children everything they desired and left others to starve and live in abominable conditions? Why would someone who loves you unconditionally ever hurt or punish you? Why would you need to do anything to impress God?

I am full and complete in myself. I do not want anything from you! Except, to unconditionally love you and be loved by you. I do not want you to love me because I am God or because of what I will do for you. I long for you to know me as I really am. I want you to know everything about me, what I look like, what I do, what its like to be with me, how it would feel to love me and be loved by me. If, after knowing me, you feel that I am not your type, then feel free to reject me or even hate me if that is what feels right for you. I want your true, genuine, heartfelt, unconditional, unmotivated and undying love. Isn't that how you want to be loved too? We both want the same thing to love and be loved unconditionally. I have given all of you complete freedom to love or hate me, to connect or disconnect from me. Love needs freedom to breathe, to choose and to express itself. Love that is forced, demanded, expected or created out of fear is not true love. Love must be chosen, inspired, awakened through beauty, sensuality, synergy, wisdom and ecstasy.

Journal

CHAPTER 5

The God Virus: As Above So Below

Rohit: I am amazed by the speed at which religion spread throughout the world. Why did this happen? Why couldn't we stop it?

God: The Judgmental God Archetype created by religious dogma became a thought virus, which I shall refer to as the God Virus. This pernicious belief system, based on distorted thinking, has pervaded the human psyche throughout the planet for thousands of years. It can be found in every aspect of the world you live in: government, law, media, politics, parenting, relationships, ethics and cultural norms. The mind computer had projected its greatest fear onto an imaginary mythical creature called God. It then began to emulate the very thing it had created. All in one extraordinarily brilliant stroke of genius! Whether you believe or disbelieve, conform or rebel; either way, the God Virus has you in its grip. It is the norm!

Every human aspires to become a God. Just as a child models itself after its parent, the human psyche models itself in the image or archetype of God. It attempts to personify its beliefs and become some version of God. This has taken many forms amongst humans, such as becoming a heroic, powerful, brilliant, controlling God; a self sacrificing, giving, selfless martyr; becoming one with God etc.

The following are examples of the impact the God Virus has had and continues to have on the quality of human life.

Many who believed that God ordered them to live according to the scriptures created law books, social norms and traditions to control one another's behavior.

Many who believed that God was judgmental, judged and criticized themselves and each other. Consequently, judges and juries played the part of God and decided if someone was innocent or guilty of a crime.

Many who believed in the supremacy of their God derided and even fought against non believers. They willingly gave away their power to monarchs, dictators and politicians. Lovers struggled for power in their relationships. Parents demanded respect and obedience from their children.

Many believed that God punishes sinners by sending them to hell, as a result they banished people who disobeyed the law from society and locked them in hellish prisons.

Many who believed that God must be feared, allowed themselves to be controlled by police who enforced the law through violence and brutality.

Many who believed that everything belongs to God, thought nothing of claiming land, possessions, slaves and even spouses as their property.

Many who believed that God is great, competed to be the greatest, richest and most powerful.

Many believed that there is one, supreme being and as a result they ensured that every country, corporation and organization had to have a supreme leader, an ultimate authority such as a President or CEO.

Many who believed that God is good and the devil is bad, hence created certain standards of morality, etiquette and social behavior. Children were socialized to suppress their natural playful instincts in order to be good and well behaved. Women were required to suppress their sensuality and men were trained to be upright, responsible and gentlemanly.

Many who believed that there was only one God, looked for "the one," the perfect love, the one true love who would fulfill them, complete them and make their life perfect.

Many who believed that the messiah would save them from damnation and take them eternally to heaven looked for a prince charming who would come on a white horse, rescue them, solve all of their problems and live with them happily ever after.

Many who believed God was jealous, angry and unforgiving, vented their greatest hate on someone who was unfaithful and betrayed their trust.

Many who believed that God needed them to prove their love, applied the same expectation to their children, lovers, spouses and themselves. It was not enough to love someone, love had to be demonstrated, expressed and proved. Only then would it be true love.

Many who believed that God must fulfill their desires expected their loved ones to take care of their needs and fulfill their desires.

Many who believed that God was the ultimate truth were deeply offended when someone lied to them.

Many believed that God was a man, hence they allowed men to have greater power, control and wealth.

Many believed that God was conceived by "immaculate conception," therefore they idealized virginity, chastity and suppression of the sexual urge, especially in women.

Many believed that God was asexual, thus their priests advocated celibacy and restricting sex to procreation. Sex was seen as dirty and shameful. Even today, public nudity and sex are banned and punishable by law in most places. Suppression of sexuality led to perversion in the form of rape, pornography, child abuse and molestation.

Many who believed that they had been commanded to worship only one God and be faithful to him, concocted unnatural notions of faithfulness, fidelity and monogamy.

Many who believed that only the deserving would go to heaven interpreted their challenges as proof that they were undeserving, worthless or inadequate.

Many who believed that the son of God suffered on the cross for their sins, unconsciously made the martyrdom into a holy ideal. This led to the unconscious belief that the one who suffers the most and sacrifices their life for others is the most exalted and dearest to God. The unfortunate result of this was that suffering became the preferred pathway to enlightenment and the planet was filled with hardship, misery and trauma, in every conceivable form, for thousands of years.

Many believed that heaven was their eternal home and this world a place of misery, as a result it didn't matter how they exploited, defiled or contaminated the Earth. The world was only a place of transition, a place to prove one's worthiness in order to enter heaven.

Many who believed in a heaven and a hell, thought nothing of living in heavenly luxury while millions of homeless and starving people rotted in hellish conditions. They mercilessly divided the world into the rich and the poor, the haves and have nots, the first and third world.

Many who believed that they were the so called chosen ones, the saved ones or the children of God, thought nothing of forcing supposedly lesser mortals into slavery and invented a capitalistic system that exploited the poor.

Does all of this sound ridiculous, illogical and bizarre? I absolutely agree! Yet, this is how the subconscious mind responds to archetypes, manifesting outcomes that shape your individual and collective reality. The psyche of the atheist and the believer have been equally infected by the Judgmental God Archetype. Avoidance, rejection and denial only strengthen the influence of a thought or belief in the human mind. For example when you say to yourself, "I must not think about chocolate," that is exactly what your mind will focus on. The more you try to avoid something, the more it will keep showing up in your world. The Adam and Eve story and the ten commandments are testimony to the fact that the human mind cannot be tamed by telling it what not to do. A wise, compassionate, loving God with an understanding of human psychology would never set you up for failure. S/he would illuminate the way for you to understand the obstacles in your way and help you replace negative thoughts and beliefs with positive, life affirming ones, as we are doing here.

Rohit: I recently came across the following quote by Timothy R. Jennings who discovered that recent brain research has shown that "when we worship a god other than one of love - a being who is punitive, authoritarian, critical or distant - fear circuits are activated and, if not calmed, will result in chronic inflammation and damage to both brain and body," from his book "The God-Shaped Brain: How Changing Your View of God Transforms Your Life."

God: The way you perceive God directly impacts everything in your life. Irrespective of whether you accept or reject God, the influence of the God archetype is present in every aspect of your lives and must be reframed if you wish to live peaceful, happy and fulfilling lives.

In its insatiable appetite for absolute supremacy, religion unintentionally laid down the groundwork for the rampant spread of materialism, exploitation and perversion. The apparently sacred notion of dividing humanity into the saved and the dammed, the faithful and the infidels, has had a powerful impact on the human psyche. This dichotomous model imbued the faithful with a halo of exclusiveness and invincibility while giving them permission to exploit all lesser mortals who existed solely for the benefit of the clergy and the ruling class.

As religious leaders amassed wealth and created ostentatious places of worship, they inspired the wealthy to amass fortunes and live in grandeur. They were the chosen ones, the Gods who ruled the Earth, who lived in heavenly mansions and deserved to have everything they desired. The millions who suffered and died without being able to meet even their most basic needs were doomed to suffer for their misdeeds. They were given charity and compassion but nothing was done to bring them out of their hellish world.

The psyche of humanity fragmented into innumerable pieces. Each person, community, race, religion and country wanted to assert its superiority and exploit others. Discrimination became rampant. White people felt they were superior to all others, Nazis felt they were superior to the Jews, men felt they had the right to dominate women, using their wives as trophies, sex slaves and domestic servants. Kings, politicians, communists and capitalists shamelessly exploited the world's poor without guilt or remorse.

The God of religion was presented as an all powerful King, Lord and Ruler of the Universe. This archetype manifested as Emperors and Dictators who represented the ultimate power and authority of the land. In time, as absolute power corrupted the autocrats, they were replaced by ruling conglomerates such as the Congress, Parliament or legislature that would create the laws and decide how people should live their lives. Presidents and Prime Ministers were elected to be the ultimate head of state. Democracy created the illusion that the people had the power to elect their leaders. Political candidates who told the grandest lies with the greatest conviction were usually the ones that got elected. Once the politicians came into power, the people surrendered their power to them and returned to a state of learned helplessness. Every so often, in some part of the world there would be an uprising, like the French Revolution, the Russian Revolution and the numerous other protests that have followed, in an attempt to overthrow rulers and change the systems of governance. In time, governments changed, as did ideologies, but none of them addressed the root cause of disempowerment: the God of religion.

Why does anyone need to rule you, lead you, control you or tell you how to live? As long as you follow this false hierarchical model, that one being is greater than all and that one absolute power exists to tell everyone what they can and cannot do, it will be impossible to create a world where people collaborate to co-create a harmonious and peaceful life.

Rohit: You said earlier that people adopted a path of suffering because Christ died on the cross for them. I didn't quite get that.

God: Whatever you think or believe becomes your reality. Suffering was idealized by some as the pathway to saving the world and bringing one closer to God. The image of Christ on the cross, suffering for the sins of the world, became an archetype that infected the soul of humanity. The experience permeated every aspect of human life: as physical suffering through hunger, poverty, disease and violent death; as emotional suffering through guilt, shame, abuse and trauma; as relationship suffering through betrayal, divorce, domination etc. The list of pathways taken by the suffering archetype are endless. It now seems as if suffering is an integral part of life that everyone must go through. This is an absolute myth. You are not here to suffer. The path to spiritual growth, enlightenment and God is one of pleasure, joy and delight. Even when so called bad things happen they are not resisted and nor do they cause emotional trauma.

Rohit: One more thing, how do we know that any of this is true or that God is real? Where is the proof?

God: The proof is all around you and that is why you cannot see it. The bird cannot see the air it flies in, the fish cannot see the water it swims in and the human cannot see the presence of God that is everywhere.

Your beautiful smartphones, computers, houses and all the creations of humans take incredible intelligence and hard work. Would you believe it if I told you that your latest gadget was an accident, no one made it, it just came from a big bang in the sky? I doubt it. If this world could be created by accident then why can't millions of scientists create another world like it or even a blade of grass or a mosquito? With all the resources of science and technology that have not been able to replicate nature. A reasonable person would undoubtedly infer that if human creations require brilliant minds then the intellect that manifested this phenomenal world, this vast and incredible Universe, must be inconceivably greater than anything you have ever come across. However, due to the ridiculous notions about God propagated by religion, the intelligentsia rejected God and sought to explain creation by a new set of unprovable mythologies such as the big bang and its modern day variations.

Millions of scientists and rationalists throughout the world rejected religious ideology and tried to show humanity a better way, based on empirical knowledge and verifiable experiments. Their determination to remove God from the picture, to brainwash generations of children and proselytize their conclusions is commendable. Despite their tremendous success they have not been able to replicate even a leaf, a drop of milk or a fruit. They have made many artificial things but nothing that would sustain life. Yet they stubbornly refuse to accept the existence of God. I admire their tenacity, their determination and their arrogance. You must try everything possible to reject me and see where that path leads. By now, I think some of you have opened your eyes and can see that the world they have created is unsustainable.

The world created by science, religion, economics and politics will self destruct and annihilate itself. You are all part of this grand experiment and are here to witness its outcome. The believer and the non believer, the theist and the atheist, as well as those who are indifferent to both sides of the debate, have collectively codified the God Virus which will continue to destroy everything in its path unless it is stopped. If you want peace on Earth, it is imperative that these distorted notions about God be eradicated from the fabric of your society, from the DNA of your thinking and the consciousness of your soul. This cannot be achieved by denying the existence of God, by becoming an atheist or reducing God to an omnipresent Energy, Light or an omnipresent Universe. The spiritual wounding created by the Judgmental God Archetype, the God of religion, must be replaced by a healed paradigm, the Loving God Archetype. A being who loves everyone equally without judgment, conditions, commandments, fear or threats of punishment. A being just like yourself who is beautiful, fun loving, sexy and wise; a being with whom you can have a real, intimate, alive and vibrant relationship. When a critical mass of people embrace this vision, its energy will spread to the entire planet and its inhabitants. A new world will emerge. A world where people respect and love each other, serve and create for the welfare of all, support one another and share what they have. As each of you make this evolutionary leap you will create a vibrational momentum that will rapidly spread throughout the world. It is absolutely essential and is certainly bound to happen, one way or another.

Journal

God, You Sexy Devil

CHAPTER 6

God Does Not Believe in God

Rohit: People ask me if I believe in God. I find the question odd. I experience God. I feel God.

God: God does not believe in God and wouldn't want you to either. When you say you believe in something, you are suggesting that it may not be real. You might find it strange if you were asked, "do you believe in the sun, the ocean or the mountains? Do you believe in Abraham Lincoln, Gandhi or Einstein?" You know they are, or were, real because there is evidence of their existence. When there is evidence, the question of belief does not arise. When the followers of religion believe in God they do so on the basis of some holy book or a preacher. They have no evidence, experience or proof. This makes logical people and scientists reject the existence of God. At the same time, they too believe in equally illogical and unprovable theories such as the big bang and evolution.

Everyone in this world is a believer. Every scientist, philosopher, politician and everyone, for that matter, who is controlled by their mind, believes in something. The positive part of being a believer is that you are open and willing to believe anything. The negative part is that once you believe something, you become closed to every other possibility. Scientists believe that reality is that which can be perceived, measured and quantified by the senses. They then name every aspect of their perception, interpret this limited information, postulate theories and believe that their conclusions are true. This flawed methodology led to the denial of the existence of the paranormal, the extraterrestrial, the supernatural, the spiritual and ultimately of God. In recent times, scientists have accepted that matter is only energy in different vibrational states. It appears to be solid but it is not. It appears to have colors but it doesn't. Ancient spiritual teachings from thousands of years ago referred to this as maya or illusion. They understood that the world you see, the events that occur, the interpretation your mind makes and the feelings that arise, are no more real than fairy tales or movies. They did not have high powered microscopes, mathematical formulae and scientific theories and yet they understood, intuitively, the nature of reality.

Religion taught humans to bypass their logical mind, develop faith and become believers. They placed me on the altar of worship in their churches and temples. They declared me to be good, pure, angelic, divine, jealous and wrathful. They asked you to believe in me, to have faith in their messiah, scripture and religion. I cannot be known in this way. I can never be the God your world believes or disbelieves in. Knowing God is an art, a science and a direct experience. There is no need for faith or belief. No matter how much the religious try to sanitize, ritualize, institutionalize and proselytize me, they cannot turn me into something I am not.

Belief is the end of openness, inquiry and curiosity. All belief is superficial, arbitrary, unintelligent and subjective. The more rigidly a belief is held, the more close minded, blind, arrogant, fanatical and ultimately destructive it is likely to make the believer. All beliefs originate in the human mind, which is a meaning making machine that believes in its own concoctions and then seeks to influence others of the same. One who is free from the control of the mind, one who disbelieves the mind, will never be trapped by its narrow focused view of the world. To remain free from beliefs I suggest remaining open and curious, wondering and exploring, searching and creating but never interpreting, assuming or concluding anything.

Whatever you believe blinds you, creates tunnel vision, distorts perception and makes you vulnerable to charlatans. Reverence, prayers, prostrations, penance, sermons and rituals cannot save you, take away your sins or bring you to heaven. They may be wonderful tools to calm your mind and appease your guilt but they mean nothing to me. The entire process of knowing, worshipping and appeasing God is based on man made, mythical scriptures. These beautiful books, once filled with words of wisdom, were manipulated by politicians, scholars and priests who presented their deceit as the absolute truth and the word of God.

What you believe is untrue and what is true you may be unwilling to believe. All I ask is that you hear me out and then decide if I am God or a figment of your imagination. Your thoughts and beliefs will not change my reality; instead they will only affect your perception and create your own reality. I do not want you to blindly agree, accept or believe me. Read with an open mind and see for yourself if what I am saying is of any value to you and whether it will enrich your life in any way. Allow my words to seep through the filters of your mind, let them enter into your soul and touch you deeply within. Trust your soul, for it knows the truth. If you are curious and open, then my words will affirm your inner knowing and wisdom. Accept whatever feels right to your heart and reject the rest.

I have come to you in a myriad of forms, through saints, gurus, prophets, musicians, poets and writers. I have come to you through every soul you ever came across and every incident in your life. I have also come in my own special forms or incarnations and have been called by innumerable names. Yet, each time that I came to you in a manifestation that you could recognize, I found similar problems. Whenever you would come across one of these evolved souls you would get lost in their personality, become powerless and surrender completely to them. Gradually you would lose your individuality, intelligence, thinking and yourself.

Dependence on another served you well, for it promised you eternity and salvation. It freed you from taking responsibility for your own progress. It made you feel that you were the chosen one, blessed, saved, delivered and in some way better and more entitled to heaven or God than the others. This dependence on another may have felt good but is has not served you. The only teacher worth considering is one who can make you equally powerful, enlightened or wise as they are. The only truth worth considering is the one that which lights up the fire of curiosity, joy and aliveness within you and frees you from shame, fear, guilt and limitations. Using this simple yardstick you will see how none of the saviors, messengers or gurus were able to make another as great as themselves. Why? Because dependence is a crutch that weakens you, stunts your growth and limits your infinite potential. It matters little how great, evolved or close to God they are they can only show you the way. No one can carry you, save you or make you evolve, no matter what they, their books or their followers may claim.

There are many dimensions, vibrational states and energy fields, whose spectrum and frequencies neither the senses nor the mind can detect. There are multiple intelligences, sensory perceptions and processing capabilities that allow different beings to have a multi-faceted view of reality. Without making room for all of these variables, religion and science set out to make sense of the world. Religion chose to believe in God and science chose to disbelieve in God. Both paths gave rise to catastrophic outcomes. I am not asking you to believe me or anything I say. If you want to really know who you are, where you came from, why you are here, what happens after death and who God is, you must find a way to silence your mind, go within yourself, perform experiments in consciousness, experiment and experience for yourself.

As long as you believe anything, your experience will be tainted by beliefs. As long as you think you know, your mind will be closed to the unknown. As long as you think about what you do not know, what you have not experienced, you are likely to speculate, interpret and guess. However, through processes such as meditation you may have a tangible inner experience, a shift in perception, a definitive realization or an awakening. Such knowing may be beyond the purview of the mind and senses. It may not make logical sense, you may not be able to explain it to anyone, but your experience will be validation that what you have experienced is factual, true, real and beyond any belief system.

It makes no difference what anyone thinks or believes. Your soul and God exist, regardless of whether you believe in them or not. Your believing will neither make God real nor will your disbelief make God go away. Everything I am saying is experiential and provable. I encourage you be a real scientist, researcher and explorer. One who experiments with the inner, non-physical world. This fascinating Universe that lies within you cannot be known through books and teachers that speak to your logic and intellect. The mind, although immensely capable in many ways, is incapable of understanding this inner world. Through meditation practice stopping the endless chatter, criticism and conjecturing of the mind. Allow it to silently wait for you at the doorway of this inner sanctuary. Enter with your heart wide open and filled with childlike curiosity. Within you lies your soul, spirit or essence, which is the treasure that you have been seeking and unable to find in this world. Unlike your ego or personality, this inner Self is your true identity. In finding your Self you will have tapped into the source of endless peace, happiness, love and wisdom. Through the Self you will go beyond knowledge and belief to experience the nature of God, for you are part of me and I am part of you.

Be willing to take the plunge and be the guinea pig. Be ready to directly experience your soul and God. Be ready to "meet your maker" ;-)

Journal

CHAPTER 7

Call Me With Love

Rohit: We have so many names for you. It can be confusing. What would you like to be called?

God: The religious have given me thousands of names such as Allah, Jehovah, Yahweh, Elohim, Ahura Mazda, Bhraman, Krishna, Vishnu and Rama. I accept all of these because they are very powerful and describe my attributes. These are not the names of different Gods nor are they the Gods of different religions. They are all the names of the same God, the One and only God, me.

The present day favorites God, Father, Mother, Lord, Creator, Source, Universe, Light, Energy, Higher Power and Supreme Being are all generic, vague, politically correct euphemisms. They reveal how out of touch you are with me, how much you fear me and how impersonal you have made me.

It is the nature of the human mind to label, define and understand things. I cannot be known, defined or named and yet I welcome your efforts to unravel the mystery that I am. Any name you give me is wonderful and perfect. It is your creation and it is your faith that will empower it to help you to grow and evolve. Your intention, devotion, meditation and love generate an alchemical energy that makes words, books, deities and places of worship holy, by inviting the energy of God to flow through them. Wherever, whatever or whoever you ask me to manifest as, there you shall find me. I Am everywhere, but by focusing my energy into a particular place, person or object, you make it easier for your mind to feel my presence.

At the same time, keep in mind that no name of mine is better than any other, all of my names are powerful, purifying and will bring you closer to me. Accepting any name of God means accepting all names and accepting one path to God means accepting all paths. You cannot come to me by deriding or denouncing another's spiritual or religious path. All paths, religions and beliefs, all messiahs, messengers and spiritual guides will ultimately bring you to me. Judgment of anyone, for any reason, will only impede your spiritual growth and take you further away from me. I love all of you, no matter if you love me or hate me, follow me or rebel against me, believe in me or disbelieve in me. I love you regardless of your views, your beliefs or your actions. There is nothing you can do to make me stop loving you - ever!

Most of the names place me on a pedestal and make it seem as if I am greater than you. The walls of formality block the flow of love and intimacy between us. I am nothing that you are not, in fact I am everything that you are ... and a little more. So call me what you will but call me with love, for the language of love is the only vibration that I recognize and respond to. My connection is with your heart, I respond to your heart and it is only a heart full of love that captivates my own heart.

Unfortunately, those who believe I am in one thing tend to become blind to all others. Your belief in one generally makes you blind to all. If you believe that I am in one scripture then you are likely to believe I am not in all others. If you believe I am in the Church then you may believe that I cannot be in the Temple or Mosque. It is the nature of the human mind to believe that what it thinks is the truth, what it believes is factual and what it perceives is reality. Fortunately, there are many of you who have now evolved from this way of thinking and may even find it strange or incomprehensible. Yet, at the time of writing these words, the majority of people on your planet are blinded by this distorted way of thinking. For this reason I no longer wish to be limited by any name, form, place, scripture or religion. Set me free to be myself, to be everything, everyone and everywhere, then wherever you go you shall find me. The whole world will be your place of worship, everyone will be your God or Goddess, wherever you look you will see me and I will always be with you.

The deepest shift occurs when you realize that you live in a holographic Universe and that what you see in one, exists in all. The power of one name for God lies in all names, the wisdom of one scripture lies in all books, the truth of one religion lies in all philosophies and ideologies. To think that there is only one way to God is a one-way road to conflict, turmoil and devastation. All paths, beliefs and ideologies, be they religious or atheistic, are explorations into consciousness and will ultimately culminate in me, God. No one is better than any other; no truth is truer than any other and no one way is 'the way.'

When one becomes all then all become One. The microcosm is a sample of the macrocosm. A drop of water has the texture, smell and taste of the entire ocean. In much the same way, when you feel my presence within yourself or in a person, place or thing, then you will be ready to open your mind and discover the truth about me. The more that you free me and experience me everywhere, the more you will free your mind and be ready to unlock the mysteries of the Universe.

To know me is to realize that the qualities you find in anyone or anything all come from God; that love is not found in one perfect person but all people are perfect and you can love everyone; that the entire planet is your home and that your religion, race, color, education or wealth cannot define the unlimited magnificence of who you truly are.

I request you not to address me as God, Lord, Father, Source, Light, Universe etc. because I do not wish to have a formal, autocratic relationship where I sit on a throne of majesty while all of you squirm at my feet, terrorized by fear.

I am in your heart, the person closest to you, your greatest love and your truest beloved. I am in your loved ones, loving you and being loved by you, through them. Call me with the love and affection that you have for your lover, spouse, child or pet. Instead of formal titles, call me buddy, sweetheart, honey, darling or beloved.

Journal

CHAPTER 8

Listen to Your Soul

Rohit: Why have you chosen me? I do not deserve the honor of writing such a book.

God: The idea of being worthy or deserving is absurd. No one is more or less deserving than another. You are all as wise and powerful as any enlightened soul that walked this Earth. You are all pure, beautiful, powerful and highly evolved beings. Every one of you came to this world with unique talents and abilities that may not have been fully explored or expressed. I invite you to step into your inner power, brilliance and light. Trust yourself and the unlimited possibilities of who you can be if you open your mind, put aside your fears and walk into the unknown.

To see someone as more deserving than another is a mental trap. Despite its amazing powers, the mind is extremely limited in its capabilities and cannot perceive the ultimate reality. In my eyes you are all equally incredible. You are all Goddesses and Gods in human form. You are just like me and yet you are not me. You are like the drop of sea water and I am the ocean. We are all of the same essence and yet each of us is eternally unique. Although we are all One in spirit yet within that Oneness lies a uniqueness such that no two beings can ever the same. We are simultaneously One and different. You are in me and I am in you. We are God and soul, infinite and infinitesimal, dancing through time and space, playing, creating and enjoying existence forever.

I am always ready to connect with each of you. You may mentally SMS, email, or Facebook me and I will gladly respond. Using your mind computer with its built-in ultra high speed wireless connectivity, all of you have unlimited, free access to the Universal Internet which is the collective wisdom of God, or in present day language, the Google of God. Your mind is an immensely powerful computer capable of downloading spiritual wisdom, healing powers and empowering energies.

The mind is an adaptive mechanism that automatically evolves, updates and expands its capabilities. It responds according to the way you use it. To restrict it to logic and reason is the equivalent of using the latest, fastest, super computer as a calculator. There is so much more that it can do. Be willing to explore with curiosity. Ask and it shall be instantly downloaded to you. Let go everything that you know, hit control-alt-delete, empty the trash of your mind and create space on the hard disk of your consciousness. Disable any firewalls of limiting beliefs that may be blocking new information from being received. The technology to do this has always been within you but very few have been aware of how to access it. No one has taught you how to access this inner world. You must learn to take charge of your mind computer and maximize its fullest potential.

You have tremendous untapped abilities, potential and powers. You may receive guidance but only you have the power to help yourself, no one else can. Logic and reason have limited you and attachment to thoughts, emotions and experiences have throttled your capabilities. To open up to your fullest potential requires a deep trust in life, in your soul Self and God. Only when you know your self as a God particle with infinite power, wisdom and grace, then will you emerge into the fullest experience of who you are.

The journey into your fullest potential begins with silencing your mind and listening to your inner voice. To experience this, put aside everything you know, open your mind and trust the first words that come to you. No matter how odd they might seem. If you are struggling, trying too hard or feeling heavy then you are on the wrong track. The symptom of being connected with me is that you will feel light, peaceful, and clear headed. Time will cease to exist as your soul awakens to its innate wisdom. It is an art that gets better with practice. The messages you receive from me will be perfectly designed for you and will carry the stamp of your uniqueness. My words will bypass the conscious mind and download directly into your body, mind and soul. As you tune in to the subtle imprints being received, as you trust them, allowing them to unfold and install into your being, you will see dramatic changes occur in your consciousness, your energy and creativity. You will rise and evolve more rapidly than any ever before. The portal has once again opened for me to reach out to you and be heard. I have been waiting patiently for you to turn to me for guidance, support and love. I have believed in you. I have known, beyond a shadow of doubt, that one day you would be ready to move past all that you have known to embrace the unknown. I trusted that one day you would want to discover the power, beauty and magnificence of who you are and know me as I Am …

Whatever you have been experiencing up until now is a result of the known and whatever you desire lies in the realm of the unknown. The mysteries of the unknown will reveal themselves, only when you embrace not knowing. Continue to remind yourself, "I do not know". The more you stay in this unfamiliar place, the more your mind will open to reveal the vastness of your inner space. You will enter a new paradigm and create a new reality.

Journal

CHAPTER 9

Believe Nothing I Say

Rohit: I am having a strange experience. A lot of what you are saying is quite different from my thoughts and beliefs and yet it all seems strangely familiar.

God: You are feeling as though your innermost feelings, thoughts and ideas are being validated and affirmed. This is because I have been speaking to you from within, whenever you were open and receptive. There were times I spoke to you directly and times when I used someone else to get through to you. I have come to you through every person and situation in your life. I have been sending you ideas, inspiration and guidance from the most unexpected sources and through the most unlikely of people. The medium that delivered my message may have been a stranger, a friend, a family member or even a child. Each person and experience brought wonderful gifts and life lessons. They were all playing a valuable role in the intricate drama of your life, even if it seemed painful, even when it hurt and made no sense.

Rohit: Wouldn't God go crazy if he tried to deal with all of the thoughts and prayers of billions of humans? How could you possibly be speaking with all of us?

God: There are millions of beings in the non-physical world helping me. This non-physical world exists all around you and is filled with beings, just like yourself, who have chosen to be of service to humanity. They have been called angels, spirit guides, demigods etc. They are busy fulfilling your desires, healing your pain, providing you inspiration and guidance to the best of their ability and to the extent that you are open to receive. I do not micromanage or interfere. My role is to keep in touch with the bigger picture. This world was designed in such a way that no one will ever die, no one actually gets hurt, no one really suffers. Your soul does not suffer any more than a person watching a movie gets hurt by what is happening on the screen.

What you will find in this book is another attempt to reach out, as I have been doing throughout the ages. I have learnt, through many mistaken attempts, not to speak in eloquent verse or erudite prose that can only be translated, interpreted or deciphered by scholars and the clergy. In recent times I have gone global and viral. I have become tech savvy and media friendly. My words have become simple, conversational, catchy, creative and yet deeply insightful. I have been inspiring people to deliver my messages through television, cinema, books, music, poetry, art, science, technology and every means of communication available. Their only qualification was that they were open, receptive and trusted themselves.

It is not necessary that you believe or agree with me. No book or generalized message can ever be perfect for everyone. It is only meant to be a road map that leads you back to yourself. You are all in different states of spiritual evolution. Each of you needs to find your own customized truth by listening to your inner voice. All of you are the chosen ones and all of you are my beloved. As you read you will learn how to listen to me, love me, love each other and create heaven inside yourself and on Earth.

Do not make my words absolute, the law, the truth or "the way." This book is not the "word of God" and there is nothing perfect, pure, divine or definitive here. It is just a wake up call. Laugh at it, hate it, burn or delete it but do not believe what I say. Find your own "inner voice," use your brain to think and you feelings to discern what is right for you. May you be "the way, the truth and the light" unto yourself.

This book is neither academically, historically, philosophically nor linguistically flawless. It is filled with imperfections that keep the message grounded and down to earth while challenging any notions the reader might have about God being perfect and infallible. Nothing about this book is perfect because God is imperfect, the Universe is flawed and existence is meaningless. At the same time everything is perfect as it is, flawless in every way and deliberately meaningful. Both statements are simultaneously true. This is the universal paradox that is incomprehensible to the logical mind.

The mind operates within a linear, either/or, black/white, true/false, dualistic modality. Things are either true or false but they cannot be both true and false at the same time. In the spiritual realm things work on the both/and/more principle, where both opposites are simultaneously true and there is even more to be explored. A thing is therefore simultaneously true and false and much more than it seems. At the same time nothing is true, nothing is false and there is nothing to explore. There is no conclusion or finality. You are now free to consciously dance between polarities such as perfection and imperfection, order and chaos, good and evil, without believing in, or identifying with, any of them. There is only a constant beginning, an ever present curiosity, a desire to see all sides of the coin and attach no meaning to what one sees. When you train yourself in this way you will no longer be controlled by the mind. Your soul will become the core operating system of your being. The soul operates in the highest vibrational state with powerful energies that will awaken your innate greatness, uniqueness and brilliance. To operate in this realm, is the beginning of mastering human potential.

I use words as symbols, to communicate and evoke something deeper than the words themselves. My words are energy capsules and when you read them with an open mind, they will release a deep feeling of calm, clarity and inner strength within you. Though what you read may not seem easy to act upon, the energy that these words carry within them will permeate into your being, giving you the strength, inspiration and wisdom to easily comprehend and practically live what is being taught. Take your time to savor this book, think about and reflect on it. Each word and each line has great significance. If you experience agitation or unrest as you read, then you are approaching my words with your mind. What you already know, think or believe may be clashing with what is written here. Take a deep breath, switch gears and try a different approach.

This book was written in a soulful, meditative, no-mind state. You will be able to identify with and extract the greatest benefit by reading it in a similar state of openness. Allow the words and ideas to permeate deep within and open like a bud within you, revealing their beauty, showering you with their gifts of wisdom. There is a great power here to help you transform and heal yourself as well as your entire planet.

Journal

The Personhood of a Loving God

CHAPTER 10

The Soul's Heroic Journey

Rohit: Why did we come here, to the physical Universe?

God: The primary reason the soul comes into the physical Universe is for self discovery. "Who am I?" The I, in this inquiry, does not refer to a person's personality, body, likes, dislikes or even their life story. The soul comes to the physical Universe to discover and express its unique qualities and untapped potential. Just as your eyes have no way to see themselves except in a mirror, the soul has no way to see itself except through the medium of this world. What the eye sees in the mirror is only a reflection, not the eye itself. In the same way, what the soul experiences in the world is an illusion that it must pierce through in order to truly find itself. This is the beginning of the journey of self realization, awakening or enlightenment.

The soul arrives in the physical Universe in a dormant state, observing, experiencing this strange world as if in a trance. It finds itself housed within a body-mind-organism. It experiences this illusory world through a virtual egoic self created by the mind computer. Bewildered and lost, it no longer experiences its innate divinity and perfection. It becomes identified with the mind and body, with thoughts, emotions and reactions. Through experiences and adventures across innumerable lifetimes, the soul gets to see various facets of itself, some ugly and others beautiful. It is given endless opportunities to succumb to this world of illusions and untruths. It is free to reject God, forget about God, hate God and experience existence without God. Until one day, battered, bruised, lost and confused, having tried everything and achieved nothing of real value, the soul longs to awaken from its deep slumber. It realizes that what it was seeking is nowhere to be found in this world. No achievement, possession or relationship could give it what it truly wanted. The soul had to experience that which it is not so that, by contrast, it could discover that which it is. For this it had to go through various experiences. Through problems it strives to find solutions, through suffering it struggles for acceptance, through negativity it leans towards the positive, through betrayal it turns to self love, through chaos it yearns for peace, through the temporary it longs for permanence, through the futility of material acquisition it will one day find the treasure of spirit and on Earth it will ultimately find heaven. At every step the soul is challenged to push through its areas of discomfort, expand its potential and eventually discover its magnificence. As the soul expands, the Universe expands, as the soul learns, the Universe learns. As the soul struggles and suffers, so does God. As the soul discovers its true potential, so does God and as the soul evolves, so too does God. We are all in this together.

Little does the soul realize that the path to self realization is full of thorns. It must find the truth amidst the delusions created by religions, cults and gurus. The flower at the end of the thorns is found when the soul stops depending on anyone or anything. It turns its awareness inwards and, within the invisible realms of its being, it experiences that which it desired all along - itself! The search, stretching thousands of lifetimes, comes to an end when the soul ultimately returns home to itself. Only this inner most place of the soul can comprehend the nature of God. In one fell swoop, the mysteries of the Universe are revealed. The soul begins to discover the exquisite magnificence of its being. It also learns how to master the mind and senses so that it may actualize its highest potential and enjoy the creation.

Another reason the soul comes to the physical Universe is to discover its origin or God. Although, in the spiritual Universe, we are eternal lovers, in the physical realm it is necessary for us to separate, have free will and then choose whether to love or reject each other. Love cannot be imposed, assumed or forced. Love must be freely chosen. This is why I give the soul absolute, unrestricted, free will so that it has infinite choices to explore, play, do whatever it wants and face the consequences. It is free to experience all possibilities. It is never forced to obey me, worship me or love me. It is free to choose, at any time throughout eternity, if it wants to know God, be with God or love God.

My love for each of you is unending. I love you even when you deny my existence. I love you no matter what you think, feel or do.

The soul's journey is the ultimate hero's journey, the greatest quest, a grand adventure that will ultimately bring it back home to God. No matter what happens along the way, the return is alway glorious and victorious. The soul's misadventures, failings and wrongdoings are all part of the experience. It will never be judged or punished. It is free to play in this world for as long as it likes. In the timeless world from where it has come, millions of years of pain and pleasure will appear to be a momentary dream. Whenever the soul chooses to fully experience itself and God, the dream will end and, like a lotus emerging from swampy waters, the soul will emerge from the physical Universe, radiant, powerful and enlightened.

Every one of you who dared to take this journey, you are my heroes, my most precious love, my priceless sparkling gem. One day you will return home to me and we will be reunited; one day we will embrace each other, we will dance together and celebrate - You!!

Journal

CHAPTER 11

Understanding God

Rohit: For thousands of years we have been grappling with the notion of God and despite all religions and teachers we have made little to no progress. Why is it so difficult to understand God?

God: Just as the human mind cannot understand the fragrance of a flower, the beauty of a sunset or the power of music, it cannot understand the nature of God. Just as a fish surrounded by water does not know the nature of water, the human being, though surrounded by God, made up of God and connected to God, is completely unaware of God.

You can experience God but not know God. You can become aware of God but you cannot see God. You can feel the presence of God but you cannot touch God. The life force, the divine energy which sustains you, makes you breathe, move, function, think and live, is entirely beyond your comprehension and yet readily available for you to experience.

The truth about God will challenge almost everything that you believe. It will radically alter your world. Aspects of this truth have been revealed throughout the ages and, more so, during the past fifty years. I will attempt to pull together the many pieces of this puzzle in order to give you a more comprehensive understanding about God.

The truth about God is that s/he has nothing to do with any religion or scripture. God does not create, control, judge or punish anyone. God imposes no rules, commandments or standards of morality on anyone. God does not expect you to conform to his/her will. God does not interfere with the events of your life or the consequences. You are totally, completely and eternally free to do, be and create anything that you desire and experience the consequences!

God doesn't think in dualistic terms such as good and evil, right and wrong. Humans, on the other hand, have dualistic minds along with highly distorted egos. For most of you, your mind is the sacred scripture that you blindly believe, the messiah you think will save you and the God, you trust, will fulfill your desires. Like all scriptures, the more blindly you believe your mind, the more likely it is that it will blind you from seeing things as they are. To the degree that your mind is in control it is likely to let you down. When it fails to save you from the calamities of the world you may find yourself falling into a whirlpool of existential crises that could ultimately lead to hopelessness, depression, insanity or even suicide.

You are the creator, maintainer and destroyer of your personal Universe. You are the only one who is privy to your thoughts and feelings. You are the sole interpreter of your story, your reality and your private mythology. You are your own judge, jury and attorney. The physical

Universe is an evolutionary playground where you come to explore, create, manifest and experience whatever you wish. You are invited to try ridiculous extremes and explore unimaginable possibilities. You are welcome to make as many mistakes as you want and fail as often as it takes for your desires and experiments to succeed.

The truth is that you are the goddess or god of your world; hell and heaven exist within you. This is your journey. You are either fulfilling the purpose for which your soul came here, or not. When you take responsibility and stop blaming the world, people or God then you will be ready to fulfill the purpose of your soul's journey. You will be ready to understand yourself and God.

Journal

CHAPTER 12

Creating a Better God

Rohit: Why did you create this world and what are we doing here?

God: I am not the creator of the Universe. You are! God is the ultimate cause behind everything but not the creator of anything. God is the energy field in which you play or the raw material with which you create. Words such as 'origin' or 'Source' that are used to represent God can be very misleading because they seem to indicate a time or place from which everything came into being. That then leads to the idea that prior to such time there was nothing. That just isn't true! Time is a mind-generated illusion. Past, present and future do not really exist, except in your minds. On the other hand; matter, energy, spirit, everything and everyone co-exist simultaneously and eternally. "Never was there a time when I did not exist, nor you, and never will there ever be a time when we shall cease to be," says Krishna in the Bhagavad Gita. How can God be the origin or the creator when energy is never created nor destroyed, when the soul is eternal, is never born nor can it ever die? Where would I find that moment in eternity to create that which exists eternally? I would have to take that which is eternal and make it non existent so that I could then create it all over again. Why would I perform this convoluted act? Just to call myself the creator? I'm not interested! You can have that title if you like it.

You say I am the creator, but in fact it is you who are eternally creating yourselves, your world and me. You are the creators, the Gods of your own life, and nothing happens that you have not in some way manifested into your existence. Each of you is a part of God and, as part of God, each of you is a god. The child of God will be a god, just as the child of a human is a human and the child of a dog is a dog. I am the infinite God and you are infinitesimal goddesses and gods.

You are supremely powerful, but you do not believe in your own powers and have thus not truly learnt to access or use them. At every step, you have been giving away your power to everyone you came across. Whenever you devote your life to your nation, religion, family or lover you may become dependent on them and unable to conceive of an existence separate from them.

The one place where this myth is often revealed is in romantic relationships where you develop all of the above symptoms of powerlessness and dependency, find yourself devastated when the person leaves and finally somehow recover only to make the same mistake again and again.

Creation is an eternal, ongoing, dynamic process. We are all eternally creating. All creation is interdependent. Each thought, idea or invention inspires another and then another, creating an infinitely expanding web of co-creation. No one creates in isolation. We are all part of one another's creation. Through our stories and experiences. Through all of your creations, experiences, emotions and thoughts, you create God.

You heard me correctly, you create God!!

There are two ways in which you create God. Firstly, just as man was created in the image of God, so also is God created in the image of man. As your mind is, so is your God. The untamed mind is by default critical, arrogant, jealous and gets angry when people act against its notions of how things should be. The judgmental, puritanical, old man God was a mental apparition, fabricated in the image of the human mind. Almost all humans are mind worshippers, who blindly believe whatever their mind tells them, see the world as their mind sees it and act according to the dictates of their mind. The one with the more powerful and persuasive thoughts will influence and shape the thinking and actions of the masses.

All original thought originates from God and enters the mind when you are receptive and not thinking. With that in mind, open yourself to a new vision of God and create a better God so that you may create a better world. Your old God produced the world you live in. Now it is time to experiment with a new vision and create a new reality. I am infinitely malleable and willing to relate to you in whichever way you desire me. I can be formless energy or light, a being who is black or white, Chinese or Indian, an old man or a youth, a man or woman or both and anything you desire. Through your desire I get to see myself in infinite ways and enjoy the unending possibilities of my existence. The same applies to you as well, when you no longer limit yourself by your body, mind, thoughts or beliefs, then you open the door to your godlike nature and the multitude of possibilities that you can create within yourself. Together, let us co-create each other into the highest vision of our hearts desire.

Secondly, all of everything is interconnected. Each of you has a massive impact on everything and everyone in the Universe. Every experience, emotion and realization of every being in every corner of the Universe is vital data that is constantly being transmitted to the Universal Energy Field. This data causes the evolution of consciousness which leads to the recreation of God and ultimately benefits all of creation. As I evolve and recreate myself, I reach out to guide and help you do the same. At times you listen, but most of you do not. It doesn't matter. Everything about you is precious to me, every thought, feeling or deed of yours is a valuable contribution that brings us closer together.

Rohit: But you do create nature, the planets and all the life forms on them, right?

God: No, even that has been outsourced to other powerful souls whom I shall refer to as alien demigods. I will tell you more about them later. They have fun creating, maintaining and disintegrating this physical Universe. I am not directly involved. I know without a doubt that no matter what kind of ride you are going through, it will all be alright in the end. Your soul cannot be destroyed, damaged or harmed in any way. At the end of every life your soul is renewed and returns to its original glory. In the end, when this evolutionary journey is complete, we will reunite and live happily ever after.

Journal

CHAPTER 13

Who or What is God?

Rohit: We have so many interpretations and opinions about God that it can be quite confusing. Perhaps, you would be the best person to answer the question, who or what is God?

God: It is true that only I know the mystery of who I am, who you are and why you are here. I have attempted to answer this question many times in the past but, throughout the ages, distortions have crept in and sullied the truth. I shall attempt to bring clarity through simplicity.

What I state here is a spiritual fact that may not be in accordance with your existing ideas. What you understand will depend entirely on your spiritual evolution, your openness and your desire to break the mould of all that you know, think and perceive. I do not ask that you believe or agree with me. It is my humble request, however, that as you read, just for a little while, put aside your knowing, be an empty page, a blank canvas and listen with your heart and soul. Take a deep breath, loosen your mind and let the words that follow sink in without too much analysis or interpretation.

God is the source of everything and the creator of nothing. God is the greatest paradox, the truest myth, the grandest illusion and the ultimate reality. God is light and darkness, good and evil, angel and devil, everything and no thing. God is all beings, all things, all forms ever conceived and all forms never imagined. God is in everything, in everyone and at the same time, is a limitless being. This is the holy trinity.

Rohit: When you say that you are a being or a person, is that the same as when some people say, "I am God, you are God, we are all God."

God: It is true that every one of you is an infinitesimal, minute, particle of God presently in a human body. In a matter of speaking, you are all goddesses and gods. This is not what I am referring to. When I say I am a person, I mean that I, the infinite, all powerful, omnipresent, source of all that is, choose to be personified. It may seem inconceivable for you to imagine how that which is everything can also be a unique person. I will keep explaining this as you keep reading. For now let me be very clear, I have a spiritual form, I have eyes, ears, nose, mouth, a body and I look just as you do. That is why it was said, "man is made in the image of God."

As I said earlier, I am the One in all and the all in One. Allow me to explain. I am in everything, in every atom, everywhere and in all that exists. The entirety of creation is my Universal body and nothing exists that is separate from me. I am also in everyone, every creature, every being and every person. Through them I experience this vast, incredible creation. At the same time, I am the infinity of all that is embodied in a singularity. I am a unique being, a limitless, non physical, person who you can see, touch, hug and love, just as you would your friends and loved ones.

I am the Light from which the person God originates and the unlimited person from which the Light or Universe emanates. I have innumerable forms and yet those who have seen my spiritual form will see one form. That form, in time, will keep changing and reinventing itself. I have two ears and yet I hear everything, I have two eyes and yet I see everywhere, I have two arms and yet I embrace all of you. I am an extraordinarily beautiful, attractive, sensual, being who enjoys life, love and all the delights of creation.

I am all that you can think of or imagine and, if you really want to know, I am unlike anything you have ever thought or believed.

I am unlimitedly creative, innovative and expressive. I delight in recreating myself endlessly, breaking all boundaries, limitations, concepts and notions about me. With every moment I am changing, growing, expanding and renewing myself. What you know in one moment is outdated in the next. The moment you think you know me, believe in me or have faith in me, you have lost me. The moment you say that I cannot be something, you display the limitations of your own thinking.

Names and definitions only limit your understanding of me. I can be anything that I desire. Your beliefs cannot limit me, your mind cannot understand me, your brain cannot fathom me and your intellect cannot comprehend me. I am beyond imagination, logic and interpretation. I am beyond religion, science, theories and philosophies. I cannot be pinned down, labeled, defined or put in to any framework.

I want you to feel free not to accept what I am saying, to believe whatever seems right for you and do whatever appeals to you. I am only sharing my point of view and asking you to think outside of the box and experience me with an open mind. If what I say resonates with you, then accept it. Even if you agree with me, please do not twist my words to suit your convenience, for then you will only repeat the same mistakes that have been recurring throughout the past centuries. You will start another religion and create more fragmentation, which will bring about even more problems, more conflict and more wars on this planet. More powerful than faith is insight, which leads to awakening, that brings about the wisdom to experience and live your highest truth.

Journal

CHAPTER 14

The Impersonal Energy of God

Rohit: It is still quite confusing how God can be everywhere and at the same time be a person. How can the infinite become finite?

God: God is formless and simultaneously has the most exquisite, beautiful form conceivable. If this feels incomprehensible then allow your confused mind to rest and stop trying to figure it out. The mystery of God can be revealed to your soul but will remain forever beyond the purview of your mind. Allow me to lift the veil and reveal myself as I am. I shall start by telling you about my impersonal energy and then reveal more about my personhood.

The impersonal, formless aspect of God is a Universal Energy Field (UEF) that is found within the physical Universe. It has been called by many names: Light, Universe, Source, Force or Shakti. It is the place where all souls go to after death, where they free themselves from their past traumas and prepare for their next incarnation in physical form. This Light is self effulgent, calming, healing and nurturing. Far beyond all the galaxies, solar systems and stars of the physical realm lies the spiritual Universe. I use the term spiritual Universe to differentiate it from the concept of heaven used in many scriptures. In this spiritual realm, the UEF exists in its original form as an unmanifest, pure, spiritual energy or Brahman. Here, too, there are innumerable planets wherein are found highly evolved, awakened, enlightened beings in non physical, spiritual forms. They are eternal and not subject to birth, death, aging or disease. This is our eternal home. I will speak more about this another time.

In the physical Universe, the UEF creates the illusion of physical forms by vibrating at a deliberately lowered frequency. It is the building block of all matter - quarks, protons and atoms. It is the raw, primal, essence that pervades everything manifest and unmanifest. It is a formless energy that takes on infinite forms. It is spirit appearing as matter, God appearing as nature, the elements and all creatures, as well as all creations. It is the force that creates, maintains and disintegrates existence. It is dynamic, constantly changing, evolving and growing. It gives form, power and ability to every object and organism. It is the all pervading, eternal miracle that makes your heart beat, that makes you stand, move, breathe, think and create.

The Universal Energy Field (UEF) is highly conscious, aware, dynamic, creative, adaptable and all-knowing. All information about everything that occurs within the Universe is stored within it, just as data is presently stored in computers that are interconnected through the internet. You may consider this to be a kind of Universal Internet (UI) that is all pervasive, everywhere, in everything and everyone. The soul is the portal through which you may access it. To access the soul, the mind computer must be silent, its firewalls must stop blocking you and its ports must be ready to receive the incoming spiritual data. The data from the Universal Internet is the source of all inspiration, creativity and wisdom, all pleasure, passion and fulfillment, all peace, joy and love. It is what you have been looking for in everything that you do. It is the key to the actualization of your highest potential and your personal greatness.

The Universal Energy Field is all around you, within you and in everything you encounter. Due to being absorbed with the mind, you are not aware of it. Presence reveals its presence. By that I mean, when you are present to your body, nature, a person or a thing, then you are transported into this alternate reality. Presence instantly connects you with the UEF. The most natural and easily accessible vehicle to get there is your breath. When you follow your breath into your body you are released from the hypnotic grip of your mind. The body serves as an antenna through which you perceive the UEF. The more present you are to your breath, the more silent your mind will be and the more you will experience a heightened sensory awareness. In this state, you will notice and take delight in things you were oblivious to before. You will have the clarity to perceive things with greater sensitivity, acuity and intuition. Your intellect and creativity will become heightened. You will feel an aliveness, a joyfulness and a loving Oneness with everything and everyone. You will be in the presence of God. You will be in heaven right here and now. Heaven is not a place out there. It is the Universal Energy Field that pervades all matter and all of life. As soon as your mental thought barriers come down, you are immediately transported into this magical world.

Besides being in everything and everywhere, God is also in everyone. I am present alongside every soul in every body. Sort of like your instant messengers or communication apps that are always connected to the internet, but a lot more advanced and personalized. This tiny part of me (call it the Super Soul, Holy Ghost, Conscience or whatever you will) sits besides your soul, holds your hand, is your best friend and tries to guide and comfort you through all of your experiences. I have always been right next to you, closer than anyone can ever be, holding you, loving you, waiting for you to listen to me as I have listened to you through the ages, waiting to revive our relationship, waiting for us to be in love again.

Journal

CHAPTER 15

Individuated Oneness

Rohit: What does it mean that we are all One? If you are God then how can all of us be God?

God: The logic is simple. The child of a dog is a dog, so the child of a God is also a God. You are all Godlike in your soul, your essence, your true Self. You have all of my qualities. Yet I am the infinite and you are infinitesimal. This does not mean that I am great and you are small, that I am all powerful and you are powerless, that I am all knowing and you know nothing.

We are One and also uniquely different. We are deeply interconnected yet totally independent, the same in spirit yet vastly different in capability. You are all God particles, infinitesimal consciousness, microcosmic Gods having human experiences on the stage of life. I am the source of all, infinite consciousness, creating, experiencing and evolving through innumerable souls, in endless universes, throughout eternity. You are like the cells in my body, like electrons in an atom, like drops of water in an ocean, like computers connected to the vast internet. You are significant, perfect, magnificent, whole and complete in every way. In your insignificance lies your significance. I have created infinitesimal, microscopic Gods with infinitely expanding potential and limitless scope for evolution.

I am the vital force that keeps you alive, makes your heart beat and keeps your energy moving. We have existed eternally. I am always with you. We have been together since the beginning of time. That expression is highly inaccurate since, really there is no time nor a beginning to our existence. Never was there a time when we did not exist nor will there ever be a time when we shall cease to be. We have been constantly interconnected, co-creating, co-experiencing and co-enjoying one another's realities eternally. No one created anyone, no one is controlling anyone, no one is lord, master, supreme or above anyone. I am the source and you are the infinite expressions of our limitless possibilities.

Let's take it one step further, not only am I in every atom of this creation, you are too. Just as every particle of a hologram contains within it the entire image, so also, do you contain within your soul the essence of God. Your soul is qualitatively the same as God. That makes you the ultimate miracle of miniaturization: a God particle that is smaller than the smallest subatomic particle and contains within it the qualities of the infinite. You are insignificant yet powerful beyond your wildest imagination. You are a God/dess! Mind blowing? That's right! All we need to do is blow your mind to pieces and out comes your soul, the authentic, phenomenal, magical YOU.

When you give birth to children they come into this world through your body but you do not create their bodies with your own hands. Their souls existed before they came into the womb and will exist even after they die. After birth you may try to guide them but it is their choice to receive or reject your inputs. Each child is always free to conform, to rebel, to love or to hate. In much the same way, while you come from me and are like me, I did not create you nor do I control what you do. You have absolute freedom to be, do and create anything you desire. Nothing you do will ever be wrong. You will never be punished, rejected or abandoned by me. I will always love, cherish, value and hold you in the highest esteem. This analogy does not mean that I am your parent. My relationship with you is whatever you choose it to be. We are always free to relate to each other in any way we desire. If you choose for me to be non-existent then I shall appear to have vanished from your life. If you choose to relate to me as an old man, a light or a darkness, then I shall be whatever you need me to be. However you choose or refuse to be with me will be the doorway through which you experience me. All doors lead to me, all paths bring you to me, for there is nowhere that I am not.

Rohit: Some gurus claim that Brahman, the Light, the Universe or Source is the origin of the being God. According to them, Avatars or incarnations of God come from the Light to Earth from time to time and then ultimately return and merge back into the Light. Yet others say that the being God is the source of the Light or the Universe. Which of these is true?

God: None of these statements are correct. Does the sun incarnate every day and merge into the ocean at night? Does the ocean give birth to the sun? When someone tries to understand me through the lens of time, they will see beginnings and endings, incarnations and disappearances, birth and death. Both the formless energy and the being God are simultaneously and eternally existent in a dimension that is beyond time and space. They may make themselves visible to us or disappear from our sight but that does not mean that they are born or that they die.

God is simultaneously everything and nothing, everywhere and nowhere, everyone and no one. God is One and all, being and non-being, form and formless, the infinity and the zero, the only reality and the greatest illusion, the absolute truth and the ultimate paradox.

God is Individuated Oneness. Waves rise and fall, seasons change and nature morphs, lovers unite and part, fortunes are created and destroyed, birth and death weave their endless spell, as the forces of change dance in and out of life. In God all opposites unite, duality dissolves, time and space become endless and nothing is what it seems … ever. Do not try to make sense of this. Behold, observe, be fascinated and rejoice. There is nothing to be done except to embrace life, as it is, and enjoy it in all of its glory.

When all opposites unite, there is only Oneness. In this state of being there is no separation, no me and you, us and them, here and there, mine and yours. As a result there is no conflict, greed, jealousy, fear or struggle. There is only peace, sharing, openness, freedom, joy, aliveness, enjoyment and love. This state of Oneness is attainable for everyone. You experience it when you fall in love, when you melt into each others arms, merge into each others eyes or crescendo into orgasm. You may also experience this Oneness when you are amongst nature, during meditation, while listening to music or at times when you are thinking of nothing at all.

Journal

CHAPTER 16

I Am All

God: I spoke earlier about how distorted notions about God have become an intrinsic part of your day-to-day lives. Let us consider a couple of examples where humans tried to play with these concepts of oneness and individuality. Communism focused on making oneness predominant. It made the state, the collective, all important and the individual unimportant. This belief system brought about the suppression of the freedom, liberties and rights of the individual, which resulted in a reign of terror accompanied by large scale killing, torture and imprisonment of those who tried to retain their individuality. On the other hand, Capitalism crated an environment where people live for themselves, their family or their nation and oneness becomes secondary to the individual. This resulted in an egotistical "me" culture, where everything from the environment to world peace and poverty were sidelined in the pursuit of profit, wealth and selfish pleasures. In hindsight, it may be observed that both of these systems lead to imbalance and destruction.

True harmony occurs when both oneness and individuality work hand in hand, when individuality leads to oneness and togetherness encourages uniqueness. Consider a society that fosters individual self expression and creativity while simultaneously nurturing interdependence and collaboration. In an intimate relationship it would mean merging and losing yourself in each other for a while and then returning to your individuality, energized and ready to be more of who you are. Without this symbiotic relationship between the part and the whole, the I and the all, me and you, it is very likely that you will give rise to fragmentation and chaos.

Rohit: You mentioned this phrase 'I am all' earlier. Is there a way to use this 'I am' principle in my life?

God: I am all is the synergy between individuality and Oneness. I am is the most fundamental truth about our existence as eternal, timeless and indestructible beings. Once you deeply understand these two words you will overcome your darkest fears, the fear of death and the instinct for survival, which is the driving force behind everyone in the physical Universe. I am is a celebration of existence, a declaration of the absolute, invincible, fearless nature of your eternal reality. I am means that I am indestructible, eternal and deathless. Take it one step further and open it up by saying, "I Am …" which means I am unlimited, open and free. Try saying it aloud. Declare it to yourself, to the sky, to the trees, let it run through you like a river, filling you with its energy of joy, the expansiveness of freedom and the thrill of aliveness. I Am …. I Am …. I Am ….. When your mind rushes in to fill the gap and asks I Am ….

what? Do not answer. Leave it wide open. I am all possibilities, I am infinite, limitless, endless, I am everything and nothing. I Am… I Am … I Am …

Lets do a little word play: I Am … is a statement of the Ultimate Reality or U.R. which can also be read as you are. I am, you are. Read this carefully: I am you are I am. I am therefore you are. You are therefore I am. You may also read it as I am you and you are I. These simple words express the deepest truth; that you and I are woven together inseparably, merged blissfully, locked in embrace, intertwined in love, inseparable and One. Your soul and God are the only truth and the only reality, everything else is just child's play, a story, an episode of your life movie. Nothing exists except spiritual reality or simply put - I am. When you place yourself (u) within me (am) it looks like this symbolically: a-u-m. This is the same as the Sanskrit word often written as om but pronounced as a-u-m with each letter stretched out to create a deep resonant sound. It symbolizes the union of soul and God, the merging of both our energies in love and fullness. Say om or a-u-m repeatedly as a mantra in meditation, remember it, experience its power to bring stillness into your mind and easily connect you with your soul and me.

When you say I Am …, then you are declaring your divinity, your godlike essence, your Oneness with God and all that is. In your physical world you say, "I am a man, I am a woman, I am a doctor, I am young," etc. There is always a label, a descriptor, a qualifier after I am. When you strip away all labels, designations, identities and personalities; when you peel away the layers of what you think you are and what others think about you, you are left with nothing except existence. Existence is all that you are: I Am …! Do not look beyond your core existence, do not look beyond soul, for in your soul, in you lies everything that you are, everything you need, everything that you desire and everything that really matters.

Your soul and God are the only truth and the only reality, everything else is just child's play, a story, an episode of your life movie. Look at every situation, challenge, feeling or thought from I Am …. Look at it with the deepest conviction that you are a spiritual being and you will see things clearly, do things effortlessly and remain unaffected by everything around you. I Am … is the key to staying grounded in your spiritual reality, keep it close to your heart and use it well.

Journal

CHAPTER 17

The Personhood of God

Rohit: Why is it so hard for many of us to accept that God is a being or a person?

God: The very notion that God can be a person defies logic. If your idea of a person is one who has a perishable human body with a physical limitations then we are both using the word differently. When I say that God is a person, I mean that s/he looks like you but has a non physical, spiritual form that can be changed at will. It is not subject to old age, disease or death; it is not bound by physical laws, nor is it limited by time or space.

Rohit: A person is supposed to have a unique point of perception. If God is everywhere then how can God see things from a unique perspective and vice versa?

God: God perceives everything and yet has a unique perspective; God is omnipresent and yet has a tangible localized presence. It is difficult for the human mind to grasp these apparent contradictions. God is not bound by the limitations of your thoughts or beliefs. The belief of the theist will not make God real nor will the disbelief of the atheist make God go away.

You may love God or hate God, accept god or reject God but avoiding or despising the elephant in the room won't make it go away. The influence of religion cannot be healed by denial, avoidance or rejection. To heal something requires that it be restored to its original, natural state of wellness.

The Judgmental God Archetype or the God Virus, has affected almost everyone on this planet. It's influence goes deep into the core of all human unhappiness and suffering. Regardless of whether you choose to surrender to or rebel from this false notion, whether you are a believer or an atheist, it has been programmed for thousands of years into the collective consciousness and DNA of humanity. You cannot escape its influence without healing it.

For spiritual seekers I have a few questions: if you are a person, then why can't the source from which you originate be a person? If you think that God cannot be a person then are you not perhaps limiting God? How is it you can imagine yourself as a God or Goddess even though you have such limited capabilities, but the Source of all, who is all powerful, cannot incarnate with all its powers if it so chooses?

To say that I cannot be something, is an absurd limitation to place on God. To think that you can be a person but that which you originate from cannot be a person, might be the ultimate egoic trap. If God is, or wanted to be a person, nothing could stop the infinite from incarnating as human. God need not take a limited physical form but may choose to appear in a spiritual form that is unlimited, perfect, infallible and immortal. Everything is possible.

For the religious I also have a few questions: why would God, who can be most attractive, handsome, sexy and alluring, choose to be an old man? Why would God, who can create the most spectacular landscapes, choose to live in some boring place called heaven in the clouds? Why would God, who created the finest music, dance and art forms, restrict him / herself to listening to angels playing on harps?

The microcosm is a reflection of the macrocosm. A drop of water from the ocean tells you about the ocean. The form and nature of a child tells you something about the form and nature of the parent. This means that, if you are a person then personhood must exist in God. The religious wounding created by the mythical God must be uprooted and replaced with a healthy understanding about the true nature of God. This maybe the next step on your evolutionary journey, if you feel called to take it.

Rohit: Tell me more about the personhood of God.

God: The personhood of God is perhaps the most delicious, beautiful and exciting aspect of God. At the same time, it is the most distorted notion about God, one that has caused the greatest damage to the planet, humanity and spirituality. Understanding the truth about the personhood of God will forever change the way you perceive love, sexuality, romance, as well as your connection to God, the world and to each other.

God is very much a person, a unique being, an divine entity. I have the ability to take on any form I choose while retaining all of my powers and potencies. I do not generally take a physical form due to the obvious limitations of the human body. Instead, I make my eternal, spiritual form visible to you. This form is not subject to birth, aging, disease or death. It is eternally youthful, intoxicatingly beautiful, extremely sensual, powerfully masculine, charmingly feminine and does not have any of the limitations of the human body. I have eyes like you, yet I can see anywhere in the Universe. I have ears like you, yet I can hear any part of creation. I am able to tap into the mind, heart and soul of any person anywhere. I can process innumerable inputs and be in multiple places simultaneously. Sounds amazing, doesn't it?! In a small way, you too have the same capabilities. You too are the God of your own Universe. Your body, mind and soul are an intricate solar system filled with infinite cells and micro organisms. You are aware of every part of your body, every itch, sensation and need that it has. Now, imagine the awe that each cell has for the whole body and for you, the soul behind that body! It is something like that.

Rohit: Why does God need to have a form and what is the value of having a relationship with God?

God: Humans have always needed a reason to come to God. They have invariably wanted something from God. This is a fact that exists across religions, cultures and ages. This insatiable need to rely on someone for sustenance, protection and wellbeing, has burnt like a fire through the consciousness of humanity. Where has it led? What have you gained? There is no value in having a relationship with God. To seek value in a relationship with another is likely to be either barter or exploitation. I am not available for either. The purpose of relating with God is to have a relationship with someone who knows you and loves you like no other, someone who who adores you, cherishes you and is there for you like no other. As for having a form, I do and I do not. I am formless and I have innumerable forms. It is almost impossible to have a loving relationship with an energy, a light or the Universe. My form exists so that you may express your love for me, laugh with me, dance with me, kiss me and make love to me.

I travel all over the Universe meeting my loved ones, being with them, loving them, inspiring them with my messages and attracting them to come back home once their journey is complete. I have revealed myself to my beloved ones innumerable times. It is very likely that I have appeared many times in your life as well. Through strangers and loved ones, I have delivered messages that touched you deeply and transformed your life. Through family, friends and lovers I have filled you with love and happiness, made you feel uplifted and excited, alive and fulfilled. In those moments that you experienced life as perfect and heavenly, you were in the presence of God.

At times I have appeared in your life as an inspiring thought, a brilliant idea, a creative outburst, a heightened ecstasy or a joyous experience. Sometimes you invited me to write, paint, play music, sing, dance or make love through you. I have even inspired you with scientific theories, brilliant innovations and technological wizardry. Whenever you reached out, I have guided you through your inner voice; through a book, movie or song; through a friend, loved one or even a stranger. You may or may not have realized that you were experiencing God. Those who are thirsty and eager to know me as I am will feel my presence, hear my guidance and ultimately, as they develop pure love for me, I will reveal to them my spiritual energy form.

Rohit: Is that not how religions were created? Someone said that they had heard the word of God through a vision, an angel or a burning bush. Suddenly they became the messenger, the messiah or the guru of a new religion.

God: I reveal myself with the best of intentions, to guide you, to reassure you, to love you and to quench your thirst for me. I cannot be responsible for what you do with me. I have seen my words distorted, used to control and manipulate others. That is why for hundreds of years I have been quiet, waiting for a time, when people will be more intelligent, discerning and evolved. That time is now and you are the ones who are ready to understand me as I am.

The reason this is vital is precisely because of what you have asked. There is no one form of God, there is no one way God can be, there is no one vision of God that is is true for everyone. God has innumerable forms but this does not mean there are many Gods. It means that I appear in unique ways to each of you. Depending on how you desire to experience me and the way you are prepared to receive me. You do not need to believe anyone's experience. No person's experience of God can be true for anyone else. I invite you to have your own experience of God. What you experience will be unique to you. You may share your experience with others but do not make them believe you, follow you or become like you.

All belief leads to fanaticism. To believe anything, religion, science, medicine, philosophy or even your own mind is to become trapped, narrow minded and shut down to all else. What you believe will always limit you, what limits you will ultimately trap you, what traps you will ultimately destroy you. Be free of all belief. Stop believing anything and you shall forever be free. In freedom you will experience God. In experiencing God you will know that God cannot be put into the boxes of your knowing. God will always remain a mystery, an unknown, a free spirit that is constantly changing and expanding.

At every stage of spiritual evolution there is the possibility that you may get stuck and ensnared by your thoughts. You may think that the form I revealed to you is the only form of God, that the words I said are the ultimate words of God, that the person who saw or heard me is the only one who had that capability. You may then refuse to accept God in any other way. Such are the ways of the egoic mind. It believes its concoctions as the absolute truth. The only truth is that there is no truth, that God does not have any finite form or message. I am constantly refining, redesigning, rediscovering and recreating myself by expressing and experiencing the ever increasing, beauty, sensuality, grace and magnificence of God.

Rohit: Aren't you a bit vain and egocentric.

God: Ouch you burst my bubble ;-) To know the truth about who you are and to love yourself is not to be vain, proud or egocentric. I recommend you try it for yourself. All of you are as incredibly beautiful and amazing as I am. In admiring yourself with humility, awe and fascination you will know the truth of your being and raise your spiritual vibration. Pride or arrogance occur when there is comparison, when you think you are better then others, or when you belittle others to make yourself seem greater. Have I spoken with such pride or is it that you are not truly able to love and glorify yourself as I am doing?

Journal

CHAPTER 18

An Exquisitely Sexy God

Rohit: I know I asked this earlier, but really, how can God be sexy?

God: Why not? If you believe that God created man in his/her own image, then if you can be sexy and beautiful why can't I? Why can't God be anything s/he wants to be? Whatever you are also exists in God. Just as you are a person, so is God. If you can be young, beautiful, sexy, seductive, intelligent, funny and so on, so can God. That doesn't mean God can't be old, angry, judgmental, insecure or jealous. I can be everything imaginable and unimaginable at the same time. I can be non-existent for the atheists, an impersonal light or energy for the spiritualists, an old and angry man for the religious and a person with the most exquisitely beautiful and sexy forms for those who wish to love me intimately. I am simultaneously all of the above and, once you have freed me from the limitations of your beliefs, you will know that I am unlike anything you have ever imagined. To really know me, free me to be myself, to show up in whichever way I wish and through whomever I choose. Recognize me, acknowledge me, connect with me, relate to me and love me in whichever way I show up in your life. Look for me with all your heart and I will find you.

I am in every way like you and you are in every way like me. Take a good look at yourself and you will know me. Break the mould of misinformation with which you were brainwashed. I am not one dimensional, good, saintly or pure. I experience and enjoy every emotion, both positive and negative, and yet I choose to live a life filled with love and laughter, pleasure and excitement. I enjoy everything that is there in the Universe, the good and the bad, the ugly and the beautiful, the sinful and the spiritual.

If you like to sing, dance, party, fight, make love and enjoy life, where do you think you got that from? From me, God! That's right! God is sexy, fun loving and playful. God enjoys sex, food, wine, music, dance, art, beauty and life just as much, or more than you do. That's why you like doing these things too. We are the same in so many ways and different too. It wouldn't be any fun if we were clones of each other. It's so much nicer to have variety, uniqueness and individuality. We are simultaneously similar and different. At the core, we are all the same.

You come from me and I come from you. If I was not there where would you be? If you were not there then who would know me as God, who would search for me and who would love me? We are inter-dependent and we exist because of each other.

The idea of God being sexy is so natural, yet no one dares to say it. They are afraid it would be sacrilegious, that it might bring down the "wrath of God" and that something bad might happen if one were even to think such a thought. What I am telling you here is the absolute truth and anyone who contradicts my words is only displaying the limitations of their own thinking. It is no surprise, because for thousands of years ungodly preachers have deluded humanity and used God as the ultimate weapon for human domination. It is time to break the spell.

Rohit: I am surprised to learn that God has all our bad qualities such as anger, hate, judgment, fear jealousy, control etc.

God: All feelings are welcome in you as they are in God. Our feelings bring us contrast, character and aliveness, they are essential for a rich meaningful life as long as they do not control or define us.

Rohit: Can evil exist in God?

God: In an absolute sense, all that is good and evil exists in God just as it exists in you. The potential to be a thief, rapist, murderer, terrorist or tyrant exists in everyone. Yet, you rise above these tendencies, you train yourself to be a good human being, to be kind, loving and bring happiness to others. The potential for evil exists in you but no longer influences you. Although everything comes from me not everything exists in me. In darkness there can be light but in light there can be no darkness. Light can drive away darkness but darkness cannot dispel light. I am the Universal Energy Field, the Light of the Universe, unlimited peace, joy and love personified. I am the Source of everything and yet, in my presence, all darkness and evil are reduced to nothingness.

Journal

CHAPTER 19

The Love Trinity

God: Love of God is based on three powerful pillars, a love triangle, a divine trinity consisting of yourself, the creation and God. These pillars are anchored on a foundation of adoration, reverence and unconditional love. To remove any pillar from this trinity would cause the entire temple of your consciousness to become hollow and crumble. You cannot truly admire an artist or writer without admiring their work. Similarly, you cannot revere God without cherishing the presence of God within yourself, all creatures and the entire creation. It is through divine communion with the creation and all beings in it that you ultimately enter into the heart of the creator.

Reverence is not a one way street between a great, pure, powerful God and worthless, insignificant, sinful humans. A vain, arrogant God might thrive on the reverence of fearful humans. A highly evolved, conscious God would, however, feel most seen and validated by those who have experienced their own divine, god-like essence. Such enlightened, self realized beings would naturally seek a loving, intimate, relationship of equality and oneness with God. In such a loving relationship there would be no room for hierarchy and no one would be greater or smaller, superior or inferior, lord or servant.

Just as it is practically impossible to love a fearful God, it is also improbable to love an impersonal, formless God. It is possible to experience yourself as love, to feel the presence of love everywhere, but there is nothing that will compare with a deep, loving intimate relationship with a person. For human and God to experience the greatest love of all, divine love, we must both have forms that allow us to see, touch and adore each other; we must have bodies, faces and arms with which to hug, kiss and make love to one another. Your experience of intimacy in this world is like a shadow that tells you of its origin in the eternal spiritual realm with God. Sexuality was not something inferior that had to be transcended in order to find God. It was something divine that had to be enhanced so that you may experience God through each other, in preparation for your ultimate romance with God.

If you desire to experience my personhood, my eternal spiritual form as Goddess and God, then claim me as your beloved, love me with all your heart and I will be yours forever. Put aside the separateness, the formality and the barriers between us. Chat with me, listen to me, hug me, kiss me, make love to me, play with me, joke with me, tease me, make fun of me, get angry with me, fight with me, dance with me, relate to me.

I long to be loved for no reason at all, to be loved for who I am, not because of who I am or for what you can get from me. I want nothing from anyone, except unconditional love and acceptance. Isn't that what you want too? I am every one of you and you are every bit like me. At the core, we are all identical. The essence, the energy in all souls, including you and me is the same. At the same time we are all unique. Our perceptions, thoughts and experiences are different. We are simultaneously One and different, same and unique, connected to each other yet free to live as we desire.

Rohit: I long to be with you, in the fullest most beautiful, complete expression of all that you are. I long to see you, hear you and love you in every way possible. When and how will that be possible?

God: You will, in time. I will certainly reveal myself to you and all those who desire to have a relationship with me. For now, find me everywhere and in everyone. Love me in nature, in the land, the trees, the plants and the animals. Love me as all of the people you meet. Grab your boyfriend or girlfriend, husband or wife, child or friend. See me in them. Love them as you would love me and I will love you through them as well. I will show you the way.

Rohit: What can I do to get closer to you?

God: You need not do anything. I am always with you, always by your side, always ready to connect with you, always longing to be in love with you. Through this book and many like it, I have been reminding you of our long forgotten love. I am the soul mate, the one true love, the knight in shining armor, the King or Queen of your heart, the ideal lover that you have been searching for all your life. All your adventures in this world have added richness to the tapestry of your being and deepened your capacity to love and be loved. Our love is the greatest ecstasy, the sweetest bliss, the most intoxicating nectar that your soul has been longing for.

It hurts me to see you resist, struggle and suffer. You are not alone. Make me a partner on your journey and let us walk together. Share your joys and sorrows, your struggle and your successes with me. Know that I have your back, that I am with you through thick and thin. I never let go of you.

Journal

What The Hell is Going On?

CHAPTER 20

You Are Burning in Hell Right Now

Rohit: Religious people believe in a heaven and hell. Do such places exist?

God: There is no hell or heaven out there. Hell is a state of mind and you are burning in it right now! The uncontrolled mind ignites the fires of guilt, regret, sadness, fear and a feast of other emotions. This is not some horrible punishment that you must suffer forever. It is a choice your soul has made, to go through emotional darkness, in order to find its divinity. It is the path chosen by the courageous soul that wishes to experience that which it is not, so that it may ultimately discover how uniquely incredible it is and continue to evolve its ever expanding potential.

The hell concocted by religion was a brilliant socializing tool and nothing else.

Rohit: Many devout preachers of the Bible claim that that those who have not accepted Christ as their savior will eternally burn in hell for their sins. We know that the body can be burnt by fire but it doesn't go to hell, it stays on earth, rotting in a coffin or reduced to ashes. Therefore, we may infer that it is the soul which supposedly goes to hell. This leads us to the question, can the soul be burnt by fire? It has been an ancient tradition amongst the Romans, Greeks and Hindus to burn the bodies of their dead on a funeral pyre. Staunch believers say that these so called heathens are doomed and will go to hell. If that is true then we may safely assume that souls do not get burnt by fire.

God: It looks like you have answered your own question. Yes, it's true, the soul cannot be burnt, hurt, tormented or annihilated, ever. The physical, mental and emotional bodies of a person may suffer but the soul is untouched by external circumstances and conditions. The soul is energy and, as you all know, energy can never be created or destroyed. Energy does not suffer, feel or experience things in the same way as the body and mind. The soul is a god particle that has, inherent within it, all the qualities of God. Even the most "sinful" person is godly within and it takes an awakened being, who can see past the veil of illusion, to see their divinity. Every "sinner" is a saint in disguise, every devil is a camouflaged angel and every "sin" the birthing of an evolutionary shift.

Rohit: Is that why Christ said, "forgive them for they know not what they do?"

God: Thats right. Jesus was an enlightened master, a beloved son of God who transcended physical pain and could see past the delusions of this world. He did not suffer on the cross, he did not die to save his followers from their sins and he forgave his tormentors because he knew that they were playing their part in the epic drama that was to unfold.

Coming back to your question about hell, I think I would like to have some fun and play around with the idea for a while. Hypothetically speaking, if such a place were to exist, the so called fires of eternal damnation would not burn or affect the soul in any way. Hell would be like a walk in the park, a costume ball, a carnival or Halloween. Hell would be a Disneyland for souls, filled with painted devils in garish costumes amidst surreal sets. A grand fiesta, an exciting adventure, a land of celebration and partying amongst fire and brimstone.

Lets take a closer look at the discrepancies in this manipulative theology. Is there anything that can burn forever? An object can be burnt by fire, but within a short while it would completely turn to ashes and then fire can have no further effect on it. Similarly, if souls could be burnt, then endlessly burning them would have no effect on them. They would be burnt and reduced to ashes in a short while and hell would be out of business. As for the fires of hell, I don't think you can get fire out of nothing. To ignite a fire you would need oxygen and something that will burn, such as wood, paper or natural gas, for which you need trees, forests or natural gas refineries. But wait, those are all things you find on Earth and hell is not supposed to be on Earth! On top of which, the cost of importing combustibles and oxygen for eternity would be prohibitive. You would also need volunteers from heaven to spend eternity in hell making sure that the fires didn't go out!

The architects of hell must have realized all this and scrapped the entire project since it was too costly, unmanageable and wouldn't serve any purpose. I guess the priests and preachers on Earth didn't get that memo.

Rohit: I get the point. Can you stop being facetious? I can see that you are having a great time with this.

God: I guess you are right. I was having a blast ridiculing this bizarre hell farce, while at the same time showing you that I, too, can be frivolous and sarcastic. Lets get back to your questions then...

Rohit: I read in the Bible from the Psalm of David, "If I ascend up into heaven, thou art there: if I make my bed in hell, behold, thou art there."

God: It is true, I am everywhere and if there was a hell, I would be there too. They would have to burn me as they burn you. Always remember that, your pain is my pain, your torment burdens my heart, your suffering haunts my soul. I would be in hell holding you, comforting you, protecting you. My beloved, I will never abandon you, I am with you now and always, for eternity and forever. I want to drive away these wicked notions, these absurd delusions and let you know that, according to me, you can do no wrong, ever! You will certainly experience the consequences of your actions but that doesn't make you bad, sinful or dammed. You are and always will be eternally loved.

Right here, right now, in every moment, each of you are choosing to live in your own unique, customized version of heaven or hell. It appears as if you live on Earth but in fact most of you live in your mind and that mind is either in a hellish or heavenly state depending on how well you are managing it.

There is no stopping the pendulum of time that ebbs and flows amidst the waves of duality. The mind constantly swings between the polarities of pleasure and pain, happiness and distress, love and hate, war and peace. Getting what you want, fulfilling your dreams or proving your worth is not heaven. Happiness must turn to sorrow, pleasure to pain, gain to loss, love to grief, health to disease and life to death. Uncertainty is the only thing you can be certain about; it is the only thing that is guaranteed and the only truth that means anything. Accept the wisdom that uncertainty brings and the way you live your life will radically change.

Learn to still the mind and you will find heaven right here and now! Heaven is within you and all around you. Heaven is in your hands. Heaven is who you are! Open your inner eyes, feel its presence and you will live in heaven forever.

Rohit: What about hell? There is so much suffering and ugliness in the world? It doesn't look heavenly at all.

God: As I explained earlier, hell is not a place, it is a state of mind, a level of consciousness. The uncontrolled mind creates a hellish reality that possesses you in its grip. Every person lives in their own unique, personalized hell. No matter how much someone loves you or empathizes with you, they cannot feel the depth of your pain or bring you out of it.

Regardless of what you possess, who you love, where you live or what you do, hell is within you, running the show, turning you inside out. Its a fantastic roller coaster ride of ups and downs, trials and tribulations, victories and defeats. When something happens that you do not want, for example a loss, an abandonment, a betrayal or a death, then the mind resists what has occurred, struggles to make sense of it and fights to change it if possible. If it cannot change what has happened nor make sense of it, then it collapses into grief, depression and helplessness.

To the degree that you are possessed by your hellish mind, you will find yourself disconnected from the heaven within your soul and all around you.

Rohit: If we don't go to heaven or hell then what does happen after death?

God: I do not need to tell you that for which there is now so much evidence. Many have spoken of their near death experiences, many have experienced past life regressions and the life between lives through hypnosis. There are thousands of documented cases. Irrespective of religious, cultural or scientific beliefs, all these accounts are unilateral in declaring the beauty of life beyond death. They will tell you that when they left the body, their tribulations, attachments and life dramas all seemed unimportant. As they gravitated towards the Light that was beckoning, they experienced themselves losing any sense of form, merging and becoming one with it. They were aware of formless, light beings, welcoming and speaking to them. Some saw family members while others saw their gods or gurus, whoever made them feel safe as they went to the light. Whilst in the Light they retained a sense of individuality, yet felt loving and connected with everyone. They felt peaceful, warm, safe and unconditionally loved. They felt revived and rejuvenated and gradually began preparing for their next evolutionary adventure in the physical Universe.

In a few cases, due to strong emotions, attachments or the shock of an untimely death, some souls may linger in this world for an undefined period of time. As disembodied, earthbound souls, unable to move on to the Light, their experience is often more traumatic than life itself. They have all the desires to enjoy, relate and experience life but are unable to do so. In time, everyone makes it back to the Light and gets a fresh start.

Journal

CHAPTER 21

Dark Energy Vibrational Illusion (d.e.v.il)

Rohit: Is there really such a thing as the Devil?

God: The God of religion is the greatest devil of all. This so called God gives people free will and then judges them for being free. He takes an angel, makes him a devil and forces him to do the dirty work of barbecuing his children. He gets to look good and pretends to love everyone while secretly judging, condemning and punishing them, in this life and the hereafter. He is feared by everyone and loved by no one. Fear and love are polar opposite forces that repel each other. Where there is love there cannot be fear and where there is fear there cannot be love. Fear is the vibrational energy of darkness, popularly know as the devil. In contrast, love is the energetic vibration of God. Not conditional love that says, if you don't believe in my son or messenger or follow my orders or belong to my religion, you will be burnt in hell forever. No! That is not love and that is not God. That is the demon God of religion running amuck in the consciousness of humanity, destroying the planet, killing the people and creating hell on earth.

You live in a magical Universe. Everything you believe or disbelieve enters your consciousness and manifests physically, mentally, emotionally or in dreams. None of it is real, none of it is true and none of it means anything. Your mind gives names, meanings and relevance to things, people and experiences but that does not make them real.

That which is real is that which is eternal. It cannot be perceived by the senses or understood by the mind, it cannot be created or destroyed, it has no beginning and no end. Spirit is real, energy is real, the soul is real and God is real. The mind is incapable of perceiving the eternal reality. The mind is a an interface with the virtual reality of this unreal world. Everything you see, hear, touch, smell and experience is unreal. Everything you believe, know, think and feel is unreal. Millions of people believing something doesn't make it real. Millions of people not believing something doesn't make it false.

The devil exists and does not exist. The devil is real, but unlike anything religion concocted. The devil is a negative energy, a dark force, a software virus that was designed to infect the mind computer and facilitate the drama of human evolution. This dark energy vibrational illusion (d.e.v.il) is the default operating system, the black matter or normative force that pervades the entire physical Universe. When I refer to it as illusion, I do not mean that it does not exist. I am referring to the fact that it is a force designed to create the illusion of hellish suffering within your mind.

This dark energy exists in every one of you. It enters your mind when you are very young. It infects you with negative thoughts, emotions and reactions. It relentlessly bullies, harasses, undermines and despises you from within. It makes you feel depressed, angry, lonely, afraid and victimized. It makes you experience doubt, criticism, guilt, shame, fear, separation, anger, resentment, hate and chaos. It drains your energy and weakens your power. Like a black hole sucking out your light, it prevents you from feeling the presence of your soul or God.

This dark energy destroys self esteem, magnifies vanity, smashes achievements until even the most powerful amongst you come crashing to your knees. It takes great pleasure in manifesting the hellish experiences of chaos, suffering and destruction in your inner and outer worlds. No one is exempt, no one escapes, no one wins and no one gets out of this hell hole without learning the lessons they came here to learn. You are all its playthings, willing participants in its diabolical strategy. You are not its victims. There are no victims. Victims have no choice but you have willingly surrendered to its torments, you have allowed it to bully you through your mind and you have become its humble, obedient servant. When you allow it to control and influence you, blindly believing what it tells you from within your mind, then it will play havoc with your life.

You may seek to escape your hellish mind by over thinking, over working or excessive reliance on drugs, alcohol, food, sex, money, power, fame etc. You can run but you cannot hide. Your avoidance strategies will only weaken you and bring you more deeply under its control. Nothing of this world can protect you from it.

The d.e.v.il has the ability to corrupt the software of your egoic mind and make you do crazy things or even become insane. It does this by taking you as far away from your soul as possible, by making you everything that you are not. If it could have its way, it would want you to suffer, self destruct or die. This is not because it has anything against you. It was designed to behave in this way.

The d.e.v.il is what you make of it. Your fear emboldens it, your hate revitalizes it, your avoidance makes it come after you even more. To the degree that you do not stand up for yourself, assert your will, connect with your inner power, it will be your greatest enemy. It will haunt you until you reach within and find yourself. It will challenge you until you stand, rooted in your soul energy and embrace your divinity. It will torment you until you find your truth, your power and your light. Its job is to challenge you to find your true Self or soul, to inspire you to connect with Source or God and become so powerful that it cannot affect you in any way.

Every soul is designed to be a lover of God. Love cannot be imposed, it must be chosen. In order to choose, every soul has been given carte blanche, eternal, unequivocal freedom to do, be and have whatever it desires and face the consequences. Without freedom there cannot be free will, without free will there cannot be choice and without choice there cannot be true love. The ultimate freedom is to choose to reject God or accept God, to hate God or love God.

The d.e.v.il will take you as far away from God and make you as averse to God as you can possibly imagine. One day, having tried everything possible, you may feel a deep emptiness within, an inexplicable desire for something more. You may feel your soul waking up and choosing to understand who you are and where you came from. When that happens it means that you are now ready to find your way home, back to the source of love, back to God. In searching for God, you will find your soul Self and in finding your Self you will find God.

Just like the bad guy in a good movie, the d.e.v.il makes the drama of life in the physical Universe challenging and exciting. All the wars, murders, thefts, rapes and all the sordid things you read about in the news are done by people under the influence of this dark energy. They have succumbed to its power and have allowed it to control them. It provokes, torments and incites them with negative thoughts. And yet, it does nothing. It is not responsible for the actions, the consequences or the karmic reactions. Whatever is done is done by the person. It is only doing its job.

The media is the propaganda machine through which it boasts all of its achievements, holding you spellbound, captivated, awed, disgusted, stunned and bewildered. As spiritual beings you may find yourself wanting to shut out news, the politics and the media circus. Closing your eyes doesn't change anything. You must face the darkness without fear, repulsion or anger. You must learn to discern its energy and strategies. You must be watchful, alert and centered in your soul power. Living in denial, fear or ignorance only increases its ability to influence you.

Renouncing the world, joining a religion, praying, fasting, rituals, saintliness, piety, or goodness will not lead anywhere. Hating the devil, being angry with it or judging it will only trap you further. Its job is to bring you home, to challenge you to achieve the purpose for which you came to this physical Universe. Through its painstaking efforts, you will finally be able to truly see yourself, to love yourself as you are, to love all creation, to love everyone and to love God. It will keep testing you until you get there. It will challenge you until the end. You cannot deceive it or pretend. It is like a tough school teacher, trainer or coach. It means no harm. It is here to support you. It has a thankless job and deserves to be respected for its tireless dedication.

Everyone of you has an aspect of light and dark, God and d.e.v.il within. If you try to disown the d.e.v.il and attempt to be all good, then it gains power in the background, sabotages your attempts and brings you crashing down into the pits of infamy. This has happened to thousands of priests and good people who found themselves inadvertently doing things that were most despicable to them. It will not allow itself to be denied, despised or shut down. With the power of your soul, with your deepest trust and surrender to God, you must meet your inner devil with fearlessness. If you have done your inner work, if you have gone within and aligned with the power of your soul then you will easily be able to own your darkness, tame it, harness its energy and creatively express it in your world. When dark and light, God and d.e.v.il unite within you they will birth a powerful energy, unstoppable determination, life altering insights and the most exciting experiences that life can offer. The d.e.v.il wants you to rise in your power so that it may serve you, bless you and support you in all your endeavors. That is its service to God.

The only thing that can counteract darkness is light. Light sources, such as the sun, candles and light bulbs bring illumination in to the physical realm. Knowledge, truth and wisdom bring light to the mental and emotional realm. Self awareness, self actualization and self expression bring light to the spiritual realm.

Just as the dark sky highlights the beauty of the moon, when you are aligned with the Light of God, then this dark energy enhances, expands and intensifies the beauty of your true Self and the magnificence of God. When your soul's mission is accomplished it gladly supports you, allowing you to enjoy the fruits of freedom, liberation and enlightenment.

Journal

CHAPTER 22

God and the Devil are One

God: The moment you see God and the devil as different, you have not understood either. Everything is God. There is nothing in existence that is separate from God. God is the power, the inspiration and the source of all that is both good and evil. Good and bad, divine and sinful, suffering and pleasure, birth and death, beauty and ugliness, angel and devil, heaven and hell are all aspects of God. When you see them as separate then you are trapped in the energetic field of duality, influenced by its polarities and bewildered by its all-consuming illusions. When you see them as one and the same, when you neither love the light nor hate the darkness, then you are free from the influence of duality and the chaos of the physical world.

Rohit: Is the devil a being or an entity?

God: From time to time I have played with the idea of having an evolved, angelic soul take charge of the negativity in the physical Universe and play the role of the devil. All who attempted got corrupted by the immense power of darkness and ultimately had to be replaced. After many failed attempts, an autonomous energy field was created, similar to a computer virus, that would act independently. Its influence is spreading exponentially on your planet causing a rapid descent into unbridled chaos and devastation. This is what it was designed to do.

I want all of you to work with my beloved ones in the physical and non physical realms to stop this force. Those of you who have aligned with me have nothing to fear. My energy is all powerful and as long as you trust me you have nothing to fear.

Everything is God. If God is good then everything is good. All that is bad and ugly, including the devil, is good. To say that God is good is very limiting. God is also devilish, naughty, bad, sexy and fun loving? God and the devil coexist simultaneously and inseparably in everyone. Every murderer, psychopath, tyrant, every so called evil person, was once an angelic, pure child. Perhaps in an earlier life this person may have been a priest or a saint and now chose to experience the opposite polarity. Every so often you too may have had thoughts just like them. You too may have hated someone and wanted to hurt or even kill that person. The only difference is that the so called evil person became possessed by their thoughts and feelings while you have so far managed to resist the urgings of negativity. You never know when you might cross over the edge to the dark side. You are no different from them. Within each of you lies a Hitler, a Napoleon, a serial killer, a mass murderer, a rapist, an abuser and a devil. Within each of you also lies a messiah, a saint and a god. What you suppress within yourself must express itself, either through you or someone around you.

As long as you try to subdue negativity through fear of God or the devil, it will expand and fill your world. Polarities perpetuate. Good creates evil and evil creates good. They are two sides of the same coin. The more you try to make someone good, the greater the likelihood they will react in the direction of that which you call evil. The rise of evil in the world makes many resolve to be good. The polarities of good and evil give impetus to each other birthing light out of darkness and darkness out of light. You will not resolve this dilemma by either suppressing or expressing the good or evil, dark or light. You must learn instead to synthesize these dualistic forces within yourself.

Unless you embrace your "badness" you will continue to manifest it. Unless you accept the darkness within and embrace it with the invincible power of your inner light, it will flourish and thrive, in the nether regions of your subconscious. When you fail to love your darkness, you will live it. Your flaws, your imperfections, your desires and your demons will show up when you least expect them. When you embrace all aspects of yourself, the light and the dark, the good and the bad, then neither polarity remains, duality collapses and what emerges is the authentic, awakened, enlightened self.

Good and bad are lame, obsolete, simplistic terms that do not serve you anymore. What would the world look like if you stopped thinking of people and situations through these limiting and distorted filters? What would happen if you refused to play the mind game of judgment and righteousness? What would happen if the devil and God were to tango within you and be reunited as One?

The fundamental experience of duality is that you repeatedly experience all that you desire and all that you hate, until you learn the futility of both. In the words of Rudyard Kipling, "if you can meet with triumph and disaster and treat those two impostors just the same... yours is the Earth and everything that's in it." To be equal to both: heat and cold, happiness and distress, pleasure and pain, friend and enemy, wealth and poverty, has been referred to by the wise as equanimity. When you can find beauty in ugliness, abundance in poverty and hope amongst despair; when you can forgive those who have hurt you, love those whom you hate, exalt those who have criticized you and feel connected with those who have left; you will become free of the egoic mind and snap out of its control. It seems impossible for the mind to accomplish such a feat, but it is natural for the soul. If you tap into your soul energy all this will happen naturally, effortlessly and smoothly. You will begin to live soulfully, accept everyone as part of you and see yourself as part of everyone. You will see yourself in the world and the world within you, you will find no one to blame and nothing to regret. You will have become a divine human, a conscious being, an enlightened soul. Without the filters of duality, the dreaded emotions of hurt, pain, sorrow, fear, anger, hate and all others that have plagued you for so long will no longer have any effect on you.

The bottom line is that I am tired of all the mythical mumbo jumbo and hoopla that has been created around me. I am as real as you are. I have feelings, desires and opinions just as you do. I am not wrathful and vengeful, nor am I peaceful and calm, I have the full range of emotions. All that I ask is that you allow me to be myself, free me from these puritanical shackles and let's get together to have a godevilish blast.

Journal

CHAPTER 23

No More Blame, Fairness and Justice

Rohit: When things go wrong, when we lose our job, property or a loved one, we tend to question, "why me?" Or "what did I do to deserve this?" We find no explanation, become angry with God, blame and accuse you for our plight.

God: The blame game is an old one and the best scapegoat is God. Blame is to be-lame, for it cripples you, makes someone else responsible and takes away your power to change, learn and grow. When you blame me or anyone else, you have avoided doing your inner work of self-healing and discovery. Blame stagnates you, gets you stuck into a bottomless pit of upsets. When things do not go the way you desire, expect or need; you feel upset, disappointed, hurt, betrayed, cheated, let down or angry. You have not got what you wanted, thought you deserved, believed was right, just or reasonable. You feel that someone did something to you and you look for a victim to dump your feelings on.

Blame arises from your own ideas of how the world "should be," what people "should" or "should not" do, from notions of right and wrong, from unfulfilled needs, expectations, and desires. As a reaction, the mind computer instantly builds a firewall of blame to protect you and defend itself. Blame avoids looking at the part that you played in what happened, avoids taking responsibility for how you contributed to the problem and projects your flaws and self criticism on others. If your opinions, desires, expectations, beliefs or "shoulds" were different then you would not be upset, angry or blame anyone. Practice turning your mind around and changing the way you look at things. Believe nothing and nothing will upset you. If you don't let your mind get in the way then nothing will bother you. More succinctly, if you don't mind it won't matter.

When good things happen you take credit, feel proud and happy for your achievements. Why not when things don't go the way you want them to? Whatever happens to you is your creation, you are the creator, the God the enjoyer and sufferer of your own world. It may not make sense to your mind but your soul knows exactly what is best for your awakening.

I did not create the mess you are in so why would you hold me accountable for it and expect me to bail you out of it? You are independent and free to do whatever you desire. You are all here playing the game of life exactly as you have chosen and desired. Every action you take expresses your desire. Every desire you have expresses the challenges you face within yourself, the things you need to learn and heal. Every experience that you have has been customized by your soul to make you aware of your blind spots and weaknesses. Every situation, no matter how tragic or painful, has been perfectly designed to help you grow and evolve. If it did not hurt, you would not know. Pain alerts you, shakes you up and makes you take action. Pain is the indicator that you are out of alignment with life, with yourself and with divine order.

Everything in the Universe is moving in perfect, impeccable harmony and order. Everything is perfect as it is. When you resist this truth and resist reality or that which is occurring and try to make it that which it is not, then there will inevitably be pain. Blaming God, yourself or anyone for being out of alignment with divine order is a waste of time and energy. Instead, feel your pain and come back into alignment, acceptance and harmony with life. Allow these growing pains to sculpt you. Allow your inner wisdom to awaken and enlighten you. Allow yourself to rise and and become even more incredible than you are right now.

Life is your greatest teacher and what you have learnt stops appearing in your life.

Rohit: We all expect fairness and justice from God.

God: Who said that God is fair or just? I made no such promise to anyone! I am surely not going to start now! I do not evaluate worthiness and decide who deserves and who does not. I do not grant some people wishes and deny others. I do not favor some and punish others. I did not decide for you to come to this world. You did!

There is no fairness, justice or goodness in the Universe. The physical Universe is a customized learning environment for souls, a university with challenges and tests, lessons and experiences, all perfectly designed to support your growth and evolution. The law of karma or action and reaction simply acts as a mirror helping you face the consequences of your action. No one is sitting on judgment, settling issues, playing the moral police or dictating what should and should not be done. Do not expect me to live up to these distorted notions about God. I have nothing to do with what goes on here. The fair, just, good, righteous, moral God of religion is a wonderful fairy tale to read to your kids at night.

The truth is that you are the masters, the controllers, the decision makers and the judges. I am a silent spectator, a witness, for most of you. Silent, not because I do not care but because many do not listen. They are so controlled by their thoughts, emotions and conditioning that they cannot hear the gentle inner voice that attempts to guide them. Even those who do listen have a hard time believing me because of their preconceived beliefs or desires.

It is not that God is just, but rather God just is!

If you cannot accept or understand what I am saying or if you do not want to, then that is all right too. You may be living in a mind warp where that which is real appears to be unreal and that which is unreal is the only thing that seems real. The physical Universe seems so tangible, so real, so in your face that it may be impossible to look through the grand illusion, the matrix, the virtual reality all around you. All that you desire and have, all of your attachments and relationships, all your worries and fears, all your thoughts and beliefs, are actually based on something that is unreal. The spiritual Universe, which is the essence of everything and the only thing that is actually real, lies outside the purview of the mind and senses appearing to be unreal.

From my point of view, all that is going on in your life is as real as the dreams, as fictitious as the movies you enjoy or the computer games that you play. Why, then, would I judge you, condemn you or interfere in your play world? You are so engrossed in your past wounds and future plans, your present worries and struggle for survival, that I prefer to let you figure things out on your own. I am certain that you will turn to me for guidance when you are ready. Until then, I have given you all the space, time and facilities that you will need to figure things out and do as you please. You have complete freedom.

Whatever you are experiencing is the result of your choices, thoughts, desires and deeds unfolding perfectly as you feared, believed or imagined. The entire physical Universe is designed to support your soul in its search for new frontiers to explore, new twists and turns to your life story. All of which will help you to become the best that you can be. It's a wonderful amusement park, enjoy it, have a blast and, if you want to make the most out of it, then take responsibility for your experiences, master the game of life and quit playing the victim or blaming others.

Rohit: So, then God really doesn't judge anyone?

God: You are having a hard time believing me. Let me say it once and for all: judgment is a foreign concept for me. It is based on duality, which is an artificial construct of the human mind. I do not have a dualistic mind and consequently do not see things as right or wrong. Without right and wrong there can be no judgment, opinion or truth. Nothing is better or worse, more or less, good or bad. Your thoughts tend to be subjective, speculative and biased. I see all sides of every story. I relish every possibility and therefore, according to me, every truth is a lie, every belief is ultimately flawed, all facts are fiction and reality is the ultimate fairy tale. The known is archaic and extinct, the unknown fresh and inviting.

Your mind computer is a powerful machine that manufactures, processes and manifests your thoughts, experiences and perception of reality. As you think, so shall it to be. Change your thoughts and your world changes. Change again and once again, everything changes. Can you tell me what is real? Is yesterday real? Is one minute ago real? Is what you see or touch real? Are your thoughts, feelings and opinions real? According to me none of the above are real. This moment appears real and in the next moment it becomes a memory. Like a dream, you can't hold on to it. All matter is made of atomic particles that are so minute that 99% of all that you see is air. There is nothing around you except microscopic particles spinning at an incredible rate, producing the illusion of reality. All that you see, touch and hear is unreal. Virtual creations, spinning on a relative space time continuum. When you are alive, death seems unreal and when you die your life appears to be a dream. Ask yourself, what are you struggling for, what are you fighting for, what are you striving for? Something that is unreal! What shall I judge, something that is no more real than a dream?

God is not just, fair or good. You cannot put me in any box. Psychologists are supposed to listen non-judgmentally. If they were judgmental, how could they help anyone? Good friends, parents and teachers are those who accept you as you are. They encourage you to be more of who you are. They do not criticize or punish you. It is the quality of the wise to see the best in others and overlook their faults.

Your true self is not defined by your thoughts, opinions, personality, gender, preferences, actions or achievements. Your authentic self is your soul and every soul is unique, perfect, beautiful and enlightened. I see all your so called human flaws or misdeeds as part of a life work in progress. I see the beauty of your life story, because through all your struggles emerges a better you. I see that you are doing what you think best at any given moment. I implicitly trust that you will do whatever you think is best under all circumstances. I trust you implicitly. I trust that your actions and their consequences, will help shape your awareness. Its like watching your baby learning to walk, getting up, falling down, trying again and again. I trust you. I know that your soul knows exactly what it is doing, the experience it wants to have and it is doing precisely what it came here to do.

Journal

CHAPTER 24

Judging God to Hell

Rohit: In some scriptures it is said that, "not a blade of grass moves without the will of God," if that is so, then are you not responsible for the world's problems? Why have we been made responsible for our actions when you are doing everything? Maybe you should be sent to hell.

God: There has to be someone to blame, right? Maybe God is the real culprit. What a thought! Let me confess my crime. I love everyone equally, the priest, the messiah, the terrorist, the pauper, the thief, the murderer, the sinner, the saint, the child, the dog and the snake. They are all my beloved souls, a part of me and just like me. Nothing exists which is not me. I love myself and so, naturally, I love everything and everyone. It is true that whatever you are is because of me, whatever you do is done by me and whatever you think is thought by me. I have my own life and yet I expand myself unlimitedly and experience existence through each of you. In that sense, whatever you do I do, your sins are my sins, your karma is my karma.

In an absolute sense, it is true that nothing happens without my will. No thought, no action, no thing happens, which is not in some way desired, permitted or done by me. I take full responsibility for all that is going on here. Absolutely nothing is separate from me! Now, since nothing I do can be wrong, therefore nothing you do is ever wrong.

There is no need to judge anyone else. If judge you must, then be my judge and jury, cast your vote and decide: am I guilty or innocent? Do I deserve to be loved or hated? Will you cast me to hell or heaven, will you lock me in jail or in your churches and temples? You decide! But wait! O my jury, before you decide to judge me, before you cast your vote and crucify me. Would you be so kind as to hear my side of the story. The question to ask yourselves is this: if I do everything that you do, then how can I punish you for something I have done? How can I send you to hell for something you never did? If I am everything, everyone and everywhere, then where would I find a place outside of me where I could go to suffer your punishment? If there is no such place and if no one qualifies to go to hell, then why would I make such a place?

Ask yourself, if everything is actually done by God, why would God bring about so much chaos, destruction and upheaval in your lives? One conclusion would be that God is a fool, a tyrant or a megalomaniac. Could there perhaps be another way to look at this? Is it possible that God, who is known to be perfect, wise and loving, knows what he is doing?

I have been falsely accused. The truth is that, because nothing is separate from me, in an absolute sense I am responsible for everything. It is equally true that I do nothing at all, I have given all of you free will and am only a witness to your actions. I was only acting according to your instructions, following your orders and fulfilling your desires. By you I mean everyone of you!

In my defense, allow me to submit my explanation. There is a master plan that lies behind all that is going on in this world, one that is based on love and on wanting to help every soul achieve its evolutionary goals in the physical Universe. Under my supervision, a multi-dimensional learning environment was created where each of you could play-act various roles, create anything you wish, experience a wide spectrum of emotions, be visionaries, creators, Gods and Goddesses. A place where you could fulfill all of your desires, have fun, be entertained, as well as learn, grow and evolve in the process.

In each lifetime your soul has been designing the experience best suited for you, finding its collaborators, setting up the time frame and parameters, before being born onto this planet, or any other. It then experiences, resolves, heals, grows and evolves. Nothing happens here that you or someone else has not deliberately planned. God has nothing to do with it and yet it may equally be argued that God has everything to do with it.

This physical Universe has no substance. Although it seems convincingly real to your mind body and senses, it is a play-world, a movie set, a Disneyland for souls to experiment and explore their powers and possibilities. The game of life has been setup like an obstacle course with certain laws such as action and reaction, birth and death, time and space, duality and illusion, in order to provide a natural system of checks and balances that will keep the game exciting.

At any time, you can choose to step out of the game, stop playing and see what it really is: computer generated images or mind generated movies being projected from millions of highly sophisticated mind computers that have been given to every soul. As soon as you step away from the illusion and shut down the mind computer, you will begin to marvel at the amazing effects, the astonishing techniques, the fascinating situations, the incredible stories created by all the directors and actors (souls) whose productions are now playing on the infinite channels of this spectacular inter galactic cable TV show. By the way, there are no winners or losers, no sinners or saved, no life and no death, no pain and no suffering. There are only souls playing, creating and celebrating their infinite powers. Believe it or not!

I have waited until now for the world to become more open minded and free, for communication to spread across all borders, so that I can reach out to all of you simultaneously. The time has come for me to vindicate myself, set myself free from these baseless and false accusations and ask you to accept me for who I am. Is that too much to ask? Isn't that how you, yourself, would like to be treated?

If there is any crime I have committed, it is that I refuse the job of being the monstrosity that religion created. I am guilty of not being a wrathful, jealous, fear mongering tyrant. I am guilty of destroying all hells and heavens. I am guilty of refusing to punish people for their sins. I am guilty of loving all of you unconditionally, as you are, regardless of what you do. If not being a wrathful God means I am shirking my duty, I stand guilty as charged. If destroying your concepts of religion, morality and society is a crime then I am certainly guilty. Punish me as you see fit.

I never accepted the job of judging the world and punishing people. In fact, no one ever asked me if I was even interested. They made up their stories and theologies. Then they went about their ambitions of controlling society. The most powerful weapons were called into play: God, religion, morality, righteousness, guilt, fear, punishment, reward, hell and heaven. Scriptures were written, people were brainwashed and I was supposed to behave myself, be compliant and play my part. I refused and now they are all mad at me. They want to send me to hell. Members of the jury, I pray and appeal to your mercy, please help me!

Journal

CHAPTER 25

Using God

God: God has been murdered on the cross of religion, tormented by the thorns of untruth and tortured by prayers of senseless believers for thousands of years. They have put me in a coffin, nailed it shut and buried me with their beliefs. They have tried to limited me, capture me and use me. They have made me their genie, their santa claus, their fairy godmother who is supposed to give them everything that they want. If their wishes are not fulfilled, they assume that they are undeserving, unworthy and being punished by God. I have been quiet long enough, but now enough is enough.

I have given you a perfect world, where everything moves in harmony. The seasons, tides, days and nights, your bodies and minds; everything is incredibly perfect. In fact the perfection is so phenomenal that you have to make an effort to notice and appreciate it. How often do you stop and notice the beauty, the exquisite perfection within and all around you? What if your heart stopped beating, your lungs stopped breathing, your food stopped digesting, the air became unclean, the waters of the ocean went out of control and filled the land, the sun did not rise or gravity stopped working? What would happen? Would your wealth, militaries, governments, hospitals or scientists be able to do anything? I am holding everything together so perfectly that most of you take it for granted.

Do you stop to give thanks for every breath you take, for being alive, for all the incredible things that were created for you on this beautiful Earth? Do you appreciate the abundance of nature, the wonderful gifts of health, intelligence, love or beauty that were given to you? Do you value the opportunities that each day provides, the miracle of life and all that you have been blessed with? Most of you do not!

Millions of people worship me everyday in temples, churches, mosques, gurdwaras and synagogues. They claim to be my followers, they believe in me, they swear by their faith in me and some are even willing to lay down their lives for me. Yet, watch them, and if you were able to read their minds like I do, you would only hear them begging, complaining, pleading and bargaining for something or other. All day, everyday, that is what I get. When you have heard it for millions of years it gets very tiring. I switched off long ago. I usually never give them what they pray for, yet they keep coming back with more and more requests. I cannot figure it out. Hardly any of them ever stop to ask the basic questions, "who is God, why am I here, what should I do, what does God look like, what does God want from me, will God talk to me or how can I meet God?" They are not interested in me, only in what they can get out of me.

What makes you think I care for all the rituals, penance, hymns, chants or prayers? Why would I be impressed by your good deeds and your sacrifices? I cannot solve your problems, they are part of your soul's awakening journey, they are essential for your growth and evolution, they were created by you and only you can find the solution to get free from them. If I intervene, you will not learn and your problems will keep repeatedly visiting you in one form or another. The challenge is not to find a savior or a God who will solve your problems but rather to turn within, find the mental, emotional and spiritual cause of your problems and become free of them once and for all.

Instead of praying and asking me to solve your problems, try asking, "God, what do you want from me? What can I do for you?" I will tell you that I want nothing from you except your love. There is nothing more precious to me than your love. There is nothing I want more than to love you with all of my heart and soul. Love cannot be forced, earned or deserved. Love is a powerful, deep, unshakeable, all inclusive, all encompassing force. Love is the highest vibrational energy of God. If you ever choose to love me or anyone, you will need to learn to love as God. To love me you must first love my creation, starting with yourself, then the people and creatures around you and finally you will be ready to love me, God, as I am.

By loving yourself I mean, nurture and care for yourself, claim the talents and attributes you have been given, respect and adore yourself, romance and enjoy being with yourself. Put your self first, my dear! This soul Self, this mind, this body, these talents, were all given to you. You may have learnt to use them but you did not create them. They are a gift that you must use wisely, with humility and compassion, gratitude and reverence. Then bring this beautiful self and share your energy, your wisdom, your creativity, your attributes and your love with others. Then, through yourself, people, animals, plants and nature - love me. When you love them, be aware that you are loving me. Then you will never tire of loving, never be diminished, never be resentful and never be hurt. When you love, leave your mind, your expectations, your needs, your desires and your issues outside the door of love's temple. Come in empty handed, open-hearted, ready to serve, ready to give all of yourself.

Whatever you do for me or anyone else, do it with love. It is love that I notice, love that I accept and love that pleases me. Love is who I am, love is what excites me and love is all that matters. The true challenge that this physical Universe provides is the test of love, trust and faith. Will you believe in God only as long as you get what you want? Will you turn against God when things do not go your way? Will you use poverty, disease, death, war and all the ills of the world to prove that there is no God? Will you use pain, illness or death as an excuse to turn away from God? Will you use all of these miseries to deepen your trust, your surrender and your love for God? Will your love be conditional or unconditional? Will you use worship, belief, faith and ritual as smokescreens to bribe or impress God? Be honest with yourself. Radically honest, sincerely humble and fully in integrity, for only then will your soul awaken to a truly loving relationship with God.

I love and miss you all. I love you as you are. I love you always. I love you unconditionally, unlimitedly and limitlessly. There is nothing you can think, say or do, that will make me love you less, break my trust, betray your love or make me leave you. Such unconditional, eternal love is called soul love. This is how all souls love each other and God. We are all soul lovers. The love that you idealize, romanticize and dream of comes from your soul. Your soul remembers how it was once loved by God, who was your knight in shining armor, the One true love, the eternal, undying love of your life. You search everywhere and fall in love again and again, only to be disappointed, hurt, sad and alone. You are looking for someone to replace the love that you once experienced with God but that is not possible. You want something that no human can ever give you. Your soul is hungry for the ultimate love, the greatest love of all, the love of God. At times you may think you have found such love through a person but there is no guarantee it will last. The everlasting love that you have been longing for has always existed between you and me. It is our eternal love that you remember and I assure you that it is still alive and always will be. Nothing will change my love for you. Remember that always.

Journal

CHAPTER 26

The Futility of Prayer, Rituals and Worship

Rohit: Is there really no need for prayer, chanting, rituals, fasts or worship?

God: It is the greatest irony that religion has reduced powerful souls into weak and powerless beggars. It has taught you that only God is powerful and only God can give you what you desire. Thus, millions of people throng in places of worship, begging God through prayers, rituals, fasts, and sacrifices. They can be very persistent, bugging and irritating but I am unmoved and untouched. Why would you want to worship or pray to me if I do not grant your wishes, if I do not intervene in your struggles, if I do not take away your pain? Wanting God to grant your wishes or solve your problems, regardless of whether what you want is ultimately good for you or not, shows that you know better than God. In that case why call on me? You know what's right for you, your mind told you so and now you are pleading and begging for me to follow the dictates of your mind. This is not prayer it is manipulation! Have you ever bothered to ask my opinion before you started praying? Have you ever tried to see the perfection in what is happening?

Some situations do seem to be horrible and unfair. They make you feel frustrated, angry, disgusted, defeated, cheated, hopeless, sad etc. You may turn to God for help and want divine intervention. That is natural. I am here for you, to listen to you, to share in your struggle, to be your best friend, to hold your hand and love you through it all. But it is not for me to fix things. Everything happens according to the perfect arrangement of the Universe. All of life's situations, no matter how challenging they seem, are flawlessly timed, meticulously orchestrated and perfectly designed for the evolutionary requirements of your soul. Nothing happens that is terrible or bad, even though the mind perceives it as such. You are all souls on a grand adventure in which your soul will never die, get ill or suffer. Whatever is happening in your world, to your body or your loved ones, will pass. If you can observe the situation objectively as a soul, see the perfection and find the wisdom in it, you will transform the way you experience even the greatest of tragedies and experience a sense of awe and gratitude. If you resist your experiences and do not learn from them, they are likely to keep on recurring. If you learn and grow, they will vanish and disappear forever. In any case, no matter what you do, your soul will never be hurt, suffer or be destroyed. If you really want to find a way out of pain, suffering and misery, then put aside whatever your beliefs and thoughts are, pause for a while, breathe deeply, silence your mind and turn within. In your inner world of peace, all problems will cease and nothing will trouble you any more.

Prayer is like a phone call to God, to your best friend, to talk about the day, to share your thoughts and feelings. Do you have any friends who cry and complain every time they call you? Do you feel like taking their calls? It's the same with me. Next time you feel like calling, instead of complaining, begging, whining or telling me what to do, try something different. The prayer that really gets my attention is your gratitude, appreciation and admiration for all that you have and enjoy in your life. The prayer that touches my heart is the expression of your undying, unmotivated and unconditional love. The prayer that brings me closest to you is communion, when you share every aspect of your life with me as you would with a dear friend.

When you see that God is with you at every step, loving you, holding you and nurturing you, then trust develops and so, ultimately, does surrender. To surrender does not mean that you will now obey God, give up your will, your individuality or your desire. It means that your trust in God has deepened and that you realize that you are not alone, God is with you every step of the way, so you can stop struggling and fighting. As your surrender deepens you discover how deeply God is surrendered to you. You understand that your desires come from God and that by aligning and co co-creating with God everything can be achieved with ease and grace. As you surrender and allow God to guide your life, you will experience a deep acceptance, peace and gratitude. As you become curious and marvel at everything that is happening, you will experience miracles all around you.

Journal

The Age of The Messiahs

CHAPTER 27

Saving Humanity From Itself

Rohit: Why did we land up with so many religions and conflicting ideas about God?

God: There was a time when humanity focused on cultivating inner technologies based on body, mind and spirit. They achieved "mystical powers" that, in present times, would be considered unimaginable. Just as present day technological devices would have mystified people in ancient times. Historical records of those times have been dismissed as mythological tales. Extensive evidence exists in ancient writings from India, Egypt and the Far East. They are ignored by modern scientists and historians because they do not make sense to their rational minds. They would have you believe that humanity is at the pinnacle of its evolution. This might be true if human evolution were to be evaluated purely on mechanistic, external criteria rather than internal, spiritual growth. The end result of modern, scientific, technological and economic progress cannot be viewed outside of the context of the massive increase in human suffering due to unending wars, global starvation, economic disparity, environmental disruption and weapons of mass destruction.

Humanity is in the midst of one of the most retrograde periods ever witnessed. Psychics and gurus in ancient times had foreseen this time and referred to it as the "end times" or the "Kali yuga." They predicted endless global wars, famine, natural disasters; a time when humanity would sink to the lowest depths of depravity, chaos and destruction; a time when all that was considered good, noble, wise, healthy and sacred would be distorted. This was all in perfect order, part of the natural cycle of creation and destruction, birth and death, order and chaos.

Highly evolved beings throughout the Universe contemplated the question: could a simple, effortless process, system or technique be developed that would connect people with God and make them enlightened? Could the consciousness of millions of souls be uplifted simultaneously, effortlessly and even instantly? They concurred that challenging times required innovative solutions. Human evolution needn't be an arduous process of trial and error, struggle and turmoil, suffering and pain spread out over millions of lifetimes. There had to be a better way, a path that would allow humans to evolve, grow and fulfill their highest potential. Many ideas were contemplated. Finally, it was resolved that enlightened beings would be sent to Earth to play the role of teachers, prophets or messiahs. They would attract people through their miraculous powers, simple teachings and inspiring words. Beautiful books, places of worship, rituals, chants and songs would make the process more attractive.

Fear was accepted as the most powerful motivator for unconscious people. They would mask the loving nature of God with tales of an angry, judgmental being who could only be appeased through obedience, good deeds and sacrifice. All one had to do was to believe in the messiah and live by a few simple rules. In exchange, past, present and future would all be resolved, all sins forgiven, and entry to heaven guaranteed. It was a fabulous deal! A once in a lifetime offer! Everyone would fall for it!

A grand experiment, "The Age of the Messiahs," was about to begin. A new Chapter in human consciousness. No one knew if it wold work but it was worth a try. The Messiah Archetype was born. Once everything was in place, millions of souls from all over the Universe gradually began taking birth on Earth. Lured by promises of salvation, liberation and freedom from past karma, they inhabited every corner of the planet, over populating it and endangering its resources. Then, highly evolved beings appeared as messiahs, messengers, saints, gurus and priests in different parts of the world. They appeared at different times each with their unique version of the salvation theme. They had enormous appeal and their influence spread like wildfire across the world.

These religious messiahs were wise and enlightened souls who rejected worldly attachments and went to remote places in nature to meditate. They connected with the wisdom of the Universe and downloaded their unique message. They then brought their messages of hope, love and peace to the world. Their wisdom, clarity, charisma and devotion to God, their ability to perform miracles, heal and transform lives, along with their promises of salvation, moksha or nirvana, made them immensely popular. People began to edify and worship them as God. They became hugely popular and set about changing the thoughts, attitudes and lives of millions of people all over the world.

The messiahs and messengers did not follow any tradition, scripture or religion. They were rebels, unconventional, dynamic thinkers who broke free from the traditions, customs and ideology of their time. They were mystics who connected directly with God and shared their realizations and personal experiences fearlessly without worrying about the consequences. That is why some of them were insulted, tortured, persecuted and even killed by the priests and rulers of their time. Strangely enough, in time, their followers would torture, persecute and kill millions of people in their name!

They did not want anyone to think of them as God, worship them, write scriptures, erect monuments or invent religions to honor them. They wanted people to follow their simple teachings, love God, do good deeds and trust that they would be saved. This was easier said than done. Most people preferred to be followers, to sit back helplessly, while the messiah did all the work for them. As long as he freed them from their sins, saved them from hell, healed them, took care of their bills and finally paid their air fare to heaven, they were ready to believe anything.

As time went along, unexpected events started to unfold and the experiment began to backfire. The core message of all the messiahs, messengers and prophets had been the same. They had expressed it through their unique perspective, adapted it to the cultural ethos and social fabric of that time. To the unevolved, it appeared as if their teacher had spoken about a different God and that people could only reach heaven through him. They began to feel that their God was the only true God, that their religion was the only way to reach heaven, that they were the chosen ones and all others were doomed.

The problem was further compounded by the fact that none of the messiahs, messengers or prophets actually wrote any scriptures. They were extremely intelligent and evolved yet they deliberately chose not to put their words in writing. They had not come to teach the "word of God" or create a law-book for humanity. They did not want their words to be held sacred, immortalized, memorized, studied, debated, preached or followed literally. Had they intended to do so, they would certainly have personally ensured that their teachings were recorded for posterity. They did no such thing. Instead, they spoke their truth as it inspired them from within. They taught for that moment and had no concern to record their teachings.

News of their miracles and teachings started to spread rapidly by word of mouth. Many decades or even centuries later, attempts were made to create a written record based on hearsay, visions and dreams. Though these writings were inspired and wonderful, they lacked authenticity. In time, these semi-fictional works found their way into the hands of Kings and priests who used them to create a system that would generate immense power, influence and wealth. They creatively distorted these writings to control people for their own good and "save" them from themselves! Whatever writings supported this objective were retained and all others were rejected. They invented an angry judgmental God, a dark evil devil, the theory of "original sin" and a mythical place called hell. They then went on to tell people how to live their lives, what to think and believe. They created unnatural standards of perfection, ideals of piety, virtue and purity that were almost impossible to attain. The goal was to keep people entrenched in the darkest emotions of shame, guilt and fear. They made grand promises of salvation and liberation in the life hereafter, for which they demanded great sacrifice and surrender of personal power, thought, desire and will, in this life. These politically manipulated "Holy Scriptures" were declared to be the "word of God," brought to Earth by the one and only son, messenger or prophet of God. Those who did not follow this scripture were doomed to suffer in hell forever.

Elaborate rituals, ceremonies, traditions, icons and deities became the grandiose hallmark of worship, piety and devotion to God. Hymns, chants and festivities were introduced to bring color and variety. The grand show was on its way to save an entire planet.

The priests vociferously taught that their prophet or messiah was the greatest, the one and only true son or messenger of God and the only way to salvation and heaven. The scriptures were regarded as the unassailable words of God. All the followers had to do was to have implicit faith, follow the instructions, pay the tithing and salvation was guaranteed. Those who did not believe were infidels, blasphemers, sinners and were sure to go to hell. The faithful strove with great enthusiasm and zealousness to follow the teachings literally and convert the non believers.

Kings, Popes and priests made themselves the ultimate representatives of God so that no one would dare oppose them. They brainwashed people to struggle, toil and sacrifice their lives for their religion. If anyone contradicted these teachings they had to be crushed immediately. For this reason religion had to be powerful, well armed and prosperous. It had to control all aspects of human behavior. Salvation, instead of saving the world, gradually became the ultimate force for control, the greatest war machine, the perfect weapon to destroy one's enemies and conquer the world.

Institutions, monuments and empires arose from the simple, nomadic roots of the messiahs' teachings. These simple, unassuming teachers were declared to be God. Their compassionate, healing and forgiving ideals were twisted into doctrines of fear and fanaticism. Their words of love and hope were distorted to divide humanity and become the catalyst for death, chaos and devastation. As faith became unshakeable it mislaid perspective, became blind and lost its way. From these diseased roots, the multi headed serpent of righteousness and fanaticism was born. This vile creature injected its venomous message into every religion, turning people against each other, bringing endless waves of intolerance and destruction, contaminating the Earth with its infectious and putrid odor and killing millions of people all over the planet.

No one could have anticipated how things would actually turn out. The power of fear was all consuming and possessed billions of people on Earth. As the multitudes of believers grew, religion became the most powerful, wealthy and dreaded force on the planet. Monotheistic religions divided humanity using the idea of one God, one son of God, one savior, one messenger, one truth and one way. Each believed their way to be the "only way," their messiah to be the "chosen one" and their scripture the true "word of God." All who did not believe as they did were infidels, blasphemers and heretics. The rhetoric was so powerful that thousands of naive, simple, decent people became obsessive fundamentalists, fanatics ready to kill, rape and plunder in the name of God. To spread their doctrine and strengthen their control, the upholders of the faith resorted to killing those who did not follow the teachings or agree with them. Mass murder, torture, rape, theft and destruction became holy attributes, tickets to heaven, as long as they were done in the name of God!

It would appear that all of these events were the machinations of devious, power hungry individuals but in fact they were part of a grand experiment that was unfolding on planet Earth. The aim had been to answer the following questions: can the process of human evolution be reduced to a simple system that would work for everyone? Would belief, faith, prayer, morality and good deeds be sufficient to uplift the consciousness of masses of people? What would happen if multiple systems were to exist simultaneously? Would the different religions respect one another or be in conflict with each other? Which system would be most effective? These were questions that no one could have answered. Only time will reveal the outcome.

The outcome was contrary to what had originally been imagined. Religion caused a drastic degradation of human consciousness. Dependence on a messiah, scripture and religion made people spiritually lazy and complacent. In time they could no longer discern between the evolved and unevolved. Thus, it came to pass that greedy, power brokers became the arrogant keepers of the faith. Dressed in regal robes that disguised their inner disconnectedness from God, armed with blind faith and fanaticism, they sold their God to the masses.

The truth is that I have never sanctioned any religion, messiah or scripture. I have never appointed anyone to be my son, messenger or representative. There is no such thing as the "word of God." There is no philosophy, ideology, belief or system that will ever be able to capture the truth, the reality or the nature of God. There is no one who can ever save you, take you to heaven, grant you liberation or make the world a better place. Anyone claiming to offer any of the above may be considered a self-serving, egotistical, deluded impostor who is using God as a means to gain power and control over innocent, unsuspecting individuals. The so called representatives of God will protest and contradict me. If ever I were to stand in front of them, they would surely denounce me and perhaps even attempt to kill me.

What I am sharing with you here is only a glimpse into the nature of God. The only way you will ever know me is when you come to me naked, undefended, vulnerable and ready. Ready to empty your mind of all that you know and all that you believe. Ready to drop your fears and well defended ego. Ready to trust me as I guide you from within. Ready to allow me to turn you inside out as I recreate you as the essence of your true self. Ready to dance with me without doubt or fear, in complete surrender. Ready to love me and be loved by me with all your heart, your soul, your life and everything that you are.

Journal

CHAPTER 28

The Neo-Messiahs of Politics, Science and Technology

Rohit: What you are speaking about may be more relevant to the past but in the present the wealth, power and domination over the human consciousness seems to lie with the not so religious, the politicians, the tycoons and the scientists. How does this fit in with the age of the messiahs?

God: In time, the absurd incongruities, the horrific atrocities, the ever expanding wealth and political influence of religion, resulted in a huge uprising of non believers. This new audience birthed a fresh breed of messiahs whom I shall refer to as the neo-messiahs. They were mostly atheists and yet, had much in common with their religious predecessors. They too believed that theirs was the ultimate truth. They too were opposed to any ideology that was contrary to their thinking. They too were busy selling the dream that they had discovered the best way to free mankind from suffering, save the world and optimize the quality of human life. In the past century, the influence of the neo-messiahs has proved to be even greater than that of religion. They became the most powerful, insidious, seductive and destructive force shaping the destiny of humanity.

When viewed as a whole, it may be observed that the utopian ideal of salvation had many contenders, each claiming to have the ultimate solution to the worlds problems.

The first wave of neo-messiahs were the Ideologists. They took the form of Kings, dictators and politicians who tried to save the world by subduing and exploiting people in the name of unity, peace and prosperity. They appeared in a multitude of forms. Megalomaniacal conquerors like Alexander, Napoleon, Stalin and Hitler; empires such as the British, French and Spanish; doctrines such as monarchy, communism, socialism, marxism and capitalism. Like the multi-headed hydra, when one ideology was vanquished, another arose to take its place. They expertly brainwashed the masses with grandiose utopian ideals such as the master race, the chosen ones or the American dream, while skillfully manipulating and controlling them. They promised much and delivered little. They annihilated anything or anyone who stood in their way. They fragmented the planet into hundreds of countries. They brutally tortured, looted, raped and killed millions of innocent people. They inundated the planet with their political ambitions, their power struggles and their wars, which wreaked havoc all over the world.

The second wave of neo-messiahs were the Innovators. From the Greeks until the present day, they appeared as philosophers, scientists, engineers, inventors, doctors and computer wiz kids who impressed the world with their theories and innovations. Collectively they formed the religion of atheism and worshiped the new Gods called reason, logic and science.

That which you hate you create. They derided religion because it was based on blind faith and beliefs. In turn, they blindly placed their faith in sensory observation, deductive reasoning and empirical evidence without realizing the limitations and fallibility of these unreliable systems. The Innovators held the world spellbound as they churned out technological inventions from their laboratories and factories. Skillful marketing companies inflamed the masses with longing for their wondrous creations. Humanity was mesmerized by these magical toys that captivated their imagination, fueled their futuristic fantasies and inspired them to acquire wealth and all the glittering things it could buy. The inventors of these dazzling products became the wizards of the modern age. Some of their key inventions were the automobile, the airplane, rockets, satellites, watches, radios, television and smartphones. They found short term solutions to humanities age old problems, alleviated suffering and transformed peoples lives. It was believed that, one day, they would eliminate all suffering, disease, old age and even death. One day they would save the world and create heaven on earth. They were revered as the new messiahs and the people believed in them, trusted them and followed them. Unfortunately, as time went by, the dark side of the industrial and technological revolution began to emerge. Unprecedented levels of global warming, pollution and environmental destruction threatened to destroy the planet and do so to this day. Modern slavery was created through financial inequality as wealthy nations blatantly exploited the worlds poor for cheap goods and services. Along with all this came weapons of mass destruction, controlled by powerful, paranoid nations who spent billions of dollars stockpiling them and waging war on any nation that they feared would upset the balance of power in the world.

The third wave of neo-messiahs were the Icons. They appeared as business tycoons, actors, musicians, writers and media personalities. They could do anything, have anything and enjoy everything. They were the new Gods, enthralling the world with their power, wealth, fame and style. They would show humanity the way to fulfill their highest potential, achieve their dreams and fulfill all their desires. They were idealized, adored and envied. Many of the rich and famous had risen from poverty, they had shown the world how to turn misfortune into fortune and helplessness into power. They came with the most enticing agenda - to show the world that anyone could do as they had done and no one had to be limited by their circumstances. It seemed as if they had found the most seductive path to heaven, the key to financial freedom, release from the daily drudgery, monotony and stress of low paying, meaningless jobs. They had found the ultimate path through which all desires and dreams could be fulfilled. By worshiping the all powerful gods of money, fame and power! In time, cracks appeared and the glamorous veneer around them began to crumble. Economies rose and fell, millionaires turned into paupers, new stars replaced old ones, new fads, trends and economies morphed generations. Those who had attained monetary nirvana often found themselves unhappy and unfulfilled. They tried everything possible to overcome the challenges of time but billions of dollars couldn't buy them what they really wanted - inner peace, love, joy, hope and wisdom.

There was no pot of gold at the end of the rainbow. Those who lacked wealth and fame were willing to do anything to get it and those who had it kept on wanting more. The more they had, the more they wanted and the more fearful they were of losing what they had acquired. The treadmill was endless. There was no time to relax and enjoy life.

The truth remained an elusive mystery that few were willing to hear.

Rohit: Are you against wealth, science, politics and everything we have created in this world?

God: Not at all! I am not against anything. I am pointing out the influence that various aspects of your life have had on you. The entire focus of humanity has been directed outwards. The attempt was to keep you away from your inner world and in order to achieve this, humanity had to be brainwashed using six primary agencies: science, education, economics, politics, media and religion. Science denied the existence of God and anything non physical that couldn't be perceived by the senses. Education focused on sharpening the logical mind and systematically shrinking the emotional, intuitive and spiritual aspects of your being. Economies were rigged to capitalize on and exploit the masses while perpetuating the illusion that everyone could attain the impossible dream of greatness, wealth and fame. Politics created power structures that gave people the illusion that they were in control, while interfering in almost every aspect of their personal lives. Media created captivating dramas that would keep people glued to screens, lull them into a stupor where they had no time or energy to think, reason or take action.

In my opinion, you have done no wrong. I am merely observing the direction that humanity has taken. Wealth, science, technology and all human endeavor is a wonderful expression of present day collective consciousness. All of you came here with unconditional free will - to do, create and experience anything you desire. You have done exactly that and now the consequences are right around the corner.

As far as possible, I observe but do not intervene. I only step in when you call me, when your heart and mind are wide open, when you are in a state of surrender and humility, ready to listen and align your will with mine. My intention is to show you what what I see, to present you with options, to help you break through your limitations, to invite you to explore new possibilities that might support you in experiencing a more abundant, fulfilling and beautiful life. You are absolutely free to accept or reject my observations and suggestions. You do not need to obey, follow or even agree with anything I say. You must absolutely do whatever feels right for you. That is the only agenda you have been given. Your consciousness will guide you to do what is right for you. My only advice to you is to align with your higher self, your spirit, your soul and allow it to guide you to create harmony within yourself, with each other, the planet and the Universe.

Journal

CHAPTER 29

Alien Demigods

God: All the messiahs and neo-messiahs played their parts perfectly. Before coming to Earth they had been scientifically engineered, trained and empowered for their mission. Each of them had unique visions, talents and skills that would enable them to realize their variant of the salvation dream.

Rohit: Then you did this! You made all this happen!

God: I do not create or do anything. As the CEO of Universe Inc. I have delegated complete responsibility for creation, management, evolution and dissolution of the Universe to highly evolved alien beings that I shall refer to as alien demigods. They have been given phenomenal intelligence, powers and abilities that might appear mythical and mind boggling to most humans. They are nothing like the monstrous creatures in Hollywood movies, in fact they are extremely beautiful in appearance. Prior to the advent of monotheism, most civilized cultures such as the

Greeks, Egyptians and Vedic (Hindu) civilizations were aware of their presence. They referred to them as Zeus, Amun, Brahma, Vishnu and Shiva to name a few. They were aware of their unique powers to create, maintain and destroy universes. People prayed to them for rain, wealth, healing, the arts, sexuality, wisdom and everything that they needed. Proof of their astonishing capabilities can be found all over the Earth. They are responsible for the Pyramids, Stonehenge and many similar structures all over the world. Archeologists imagine that these ancient monuments were made by millions of workers using primitive tools. The truth is they were made by a few individuals using mystical powers that may seem inconceivable to modern, scientific ideology.

The fascination that humanity has had with superheroes, wizards, aliens and beings with extraordinary capabilities is based on fact not fiction. Heroic characters such as Merlin, Achilles, Superman, Harry Potter and others have captivated people. The reason they are so popular is because they touch a common chord in humanity that reminds you of the great untapped potential and power that lies within each of you. You are inspired and attracted to them because, at your core, you know that you too have mystical, supernatural, capabilities. You know that miracles are possible, that you are capable of far more than you can presently think, perceive or even imagine.

I have never been directly involved in the day-to-day affairs of the Universes. No one person, not even God, can possibly deal with everything and everyone. I gave these alien demigods the power to design the prototypes for all the species throughout the infinite Universes and Galaxies. They were given the task of creation, management and dissolution, to ensure the smooth running of the physical universe. This does not mean that they are perfect, infallible or that they will not make mistakes. They are as human and fallible as you are. The only difference is that they know, trust, love and serve me.

From time to time they have remotely connected with some of you. They have given you ideas, concepts and visions to assist you in creating new technologies, inventions, ideologies and systems. Their agenda was never to control things but rather to create environments and opportunities, to support, inspire and guide you, so that you may make your best choices.

Modern scientists, historians and archeologists have cultivated belief systems that have blinded them to the obvious. This too was part of the plan, to see how humans would evolve if they shut out all awareness of God, Demigods, aliens, extrasensory perception and all things supernatural. Every human was free to choose their own path and deal with the consequences. No one could accurately predict the events that would unfold in human history.

Rohit: Why were alien demigods interested in humans? What did they want from us?

God: Humans of various types have inhabited Earth for hundreds of millions of years. Anthropologists claim that homo sapiens, modern day humans, have inhabited the planet for only 200,000 years. In time they will discover highly evolved human civilizations going back hundreds of millions of years. Then their short sighted theories of the big bang, origin of species and evolutionary biology will come crumbling down. Unfortunately, the human species has managed to self destruct numerous times. Once again they stand at the edge of annihilation because they have failed to see the obvious and heed the warning signs all around them.

The demigods have been trying desperately to find a way to evolve the human species into a sustainable model. They wanted to devise a way to evolve human consciousness expediently, simultaneously and permanently. The messiahs and neo-messiahs were evolved souls who had been engineered, trained and empowered to the manifest the various experiments that the demigods believed would evolve the consciousness of planet Earth. If their experiments had been successful, they would have found a prototype that would benefit beings throughout the Universe. Unfortunately all their experiments were unsuccessful. When one religion failed, they created another and then another. When it became clear that religion had failed to achieve their objective, they tried alternate paths such as philosophy, psychology, science, politics, business and even entertainment.

The dazzling events that unfolded held billions of souls in fascination. They had taken birth on Earth to be part of a grand experiment. They had sought out great teachers and followed them. Each time a new messiah emerged with a better ideology or product, they rushed towards them like moths to a flame. Filled with hope, trust and naivety, they whole heartedly embraced their new found savior and devoted their lives to living, proselytizing and defending their visions. In time, every ideology, system, theory, messiah and product proved to be flawed. Disillusionment led to mental illness, addictions, wars, rebellions, chaos and confusion. That was, until the next ray of hope, the next messiah emerged on the horizon.

The intent behind these various experiments was sincere and well intentioned. However, instead of saving the world, improving the quality of peoples lives or raising their consciousness they only created more misery and chaos than the problems they tried to solve. Planet Earth is now filled with fanatical fundamentalists in a multitude of hues - religious, political, scientific and economic. They all believe that their ideology is superior while all others are flawed and misguided. Supremacist thinking of this nature tends to breed deep rooted feelings of invincibility, righteousness and arrogance. It makes one focus all fault and blame on others while turning a blind eye to ones own weaknesses and transgressions. The virus like disease of fanaticism, in one form or other, has penetrated into the hearts and minds of most people on this planet, spreading havoc and destruction. Irrespective of the route the saviors took, their grand visions inevitably morphed into sordid battlegrounds that led to chaos and destruction. They were not able to save the planet, let alone their followers or even themselves! Instead of improving the quality of people's lives, they created hell on Earth and brought humanity to the brink of annihilation.

The "Age of the Messiahs" has officially ended. It was a grand experiment that failed miserably. Rama, Krishna, Moses, Christ, Mohammed, Ali, Buddha and Nanak have all failed! The gurus, saints, popes, priests and the religions they created have all failed! Religion has outlived its time and has become a hazardous toxic ideology that is threatening the wellbeing of this planet and all its inhabitants.

The neo-messiahs have failed! Alexander, Napoleon, Marx, Stalin,

Mao, Hitler, Gandhi, Copernicus, Leonardo da Vinci, Edison, Bill Gates, Steve Jobs, to name a few, have all failed! They conquered, conceptualized and capitalized. They tried to save the world through power, politics, technology and money. They put on a great show and created dazzling magic but none it of it created the things that really matter: peace, love, kindness or harmony.

Rohit: I have read articles by scientists who speak of the sixth mass extinction. They predict that as many as 30% of all species may be lost over the next four decades and 75% of all mammal species will have disappeared from this planet in around 300 years time.

God: The time has come for the the human species, as you know it, to become extinct! The facts, the evidence and the truth is in front of you. More than half of the world's population now live in abject poverty. Their dreams of equality, liberty, justice and the pursuit of happiness have crumbled. People are waking up to the lies and deceit of their leaders. No one has been able to give them the quality of life that they desire. Uprisings, revolutions and protests have begun to spring up all over the planet. Mankind's disruption of the ecological balance on Earth will not only cause the extinction of innumerable species but also trigger natural disasters that will wipe out life as you know it from the face of the Earth. The Earth has tolerated mankind's exploitative and irresponsible pursuits for too long. She has begun to cry out in protest, expressing her feelings through tsunamis, earthquakes, forest fires, hurricanes and climate change. Humanity in its present state of consciousness has become a menace that will cause its own annihilation in the very near future. Such extinctions are nothing new. Over millions of years the Earth has seen humans evolve and devolve and civilizations rise and fall.

This is not some doomsday prediction. I am not here to scare you. This is only a street sign telling you that the road ahead is extremely dangerous. It is a realistic assessment of where humanity has arrived. Your world is entering into its most chaotic phase. I do not need to predict anything. The newspapers and media are filled with daily reports of war, violence, unrest, scarcity, perversion and environmental destruction taking place all over the world. Scientists, sociologists and environmentalists have declared the destruction of human life due to global warming, pollution, overpopulation, scarcity of natural resources etc.

Having said this, I want you to know that there is nothing to fear. In the ultimate analysis, none of what has happened or will happen, really matters. Just as energy is neither created nor destroyed, so also, life cannot be created or destroyed. Matter, energy and life may change forms but they can never be annihilated. You are all imperishable beings. If the world you have known is destroyed then new worlds will arise from the ashes. If life on this planet is wiped out it will reincarnate on another. A million Earths can be created in a flash and all the souls can be recycled into new forms.

The Earth will survive, new life will come forth and things will get infinitely better. One way or the other the "Age of Awakening," a golden era, is waiting to break through the darkness of winter and shine like spring, spreading its warmth and light on all. Nothing can stop the return of harmony, the revelation of truth and the relentless evolution of consciousness. In this truth lies the answer to all that you have been seeking, the resurrection of your soul and the recreation of this world as heaven on earth.

I do not mean that we should stand by and do nothing. We need to work together closely and in harmony. There is no time to think and speculate, you must wake up and take action. This is a very critical phase. You must all get involved and act quickly. There is no time to procrastinate. Use your gifts and skills to make a difference. Humanity will survive nature's backlash, only if there is a massive change in attitudes, beliefs and actions. The time has come to find an inner way, an inner technology, that leads to the core of the issue.

Many of you have opened your eyes, started looking outside the box and have begun to alter your belief systems. You have begun to explore the unknown and unfamiliar. Through science fiction, fantasy, mythology, intuition and ancient spiritual teachings you are now open to new possibilities and are ready to hear the truth. You have invoked me and I am ready to answer all of your questions. I am ready to work with you. I am ready to support you. I am ready to receive you into my loving arms.

Journal

CHAPTER 30

The Seven Deadly Flaws of Salvation

Rohit: Why did the experiment of salvation fail? Instead of saving people from misery and suffering, instead of enlightening and uplifting, why did it lead to such incredible chaos and destruction?

God: No one could have foreseen the grand drama, the horror and the suffering that unfolded and spread to every corner of the planet. No one detected the flaws in the theory of salvation. The premise of salvation had been so seductively simple, irresistible and alluring, that few dared to challenge its validity. The goal had been so compelling, powerful and altruistic that they were convinced it would be a grand success. The obvious, though, was invisible; veiled behind sincere intentions, noble ideals and compassionate hearts. I tried to intervene but no one was listening. The consequences of their experiment would be revealed in time but by then it would be too late.

Despite the setbacks and failures, the dream of instant salvation is still alive and deeply imbedded in the human psyche. Any scheme that promises to solve people's problems and any secret that will fulfill their dreams, still sells like hot cakes. Its big business! Those who have understood how to manipulate human desire have amassed enormous wealth, power and prestige. They will do everything to prevent things from changing. The irony is, that which you avoid you will attract, that which you suppress will persist and that which you hate you will become.

Salvation cannot solve anything. Dreams may seduce you to escape your current reality but they will inevitably bring you back to where you started. Changing your outer world will never change your inner world. Transformation occurs from the inside out, from your inner world to your outer world and from consciousness to manifestation. Your consciousness will show up wherever you are. It cannot be masked, hidden or avoided. Your reality will only change when your consciousness changes. Attracting or manifesting your desires will not change the way you experience the world. The scenario will change, the movie set will change but the script will go on.

To get back to your question, there are basically two answers to why the experiment of salvation failed: the inherent flaws in the theory of salvation and the curse of righteousness. First let us examine the flaws.

The first flaw: the contract.

Traditional religious and spiritual teachings point out that the world is a place of suffering and the human body is inevitably subject to disease, old age and death. They go on to preach that the the ultimate solution to the miseries of the world is salvation, liberation, moksha and nirvana which are achieved by returning to the light or heaven. (This reminds me of a salesman who first magnifies the problem, establishes the need for a solution and then offers to sell his product as the best and perhaps only alternative). They then propose that ideally one should renounce or minimize bodily pleasures, give as much of one's wealth to charity and devote as much of one's time to serve others, rather than to selfish pursuits. This entire line of thought is based on mentally concocted, fear induced thinking. There is nothing spiritual in this perspective.

The reality is that this "material world" or physical Universe, with all its planets, galaxies and solar systems, was designed for an amazing purpose. It is the most incredible place of learning ever created. Souls voluntarily come here to evolve and grow through a learning process that is based on three dimensional, hands-on, situational experiments. These life experiments, or experiences as you call them, are designed to explore a wide range of issues such as love, lust, jealousy, power, victimization, abuse, death, genocide, loss, poverty etc. Souls choose to play various parts in the drama of life, interacting with other souls by emotionally triggering in them the very reactions that they seek to work on. No one dies, gets hurt or is actually harmed. There are no bad or good guys. Everyone evolves and benefits from their self-created experiments, no matter how bizarre, painful or tragic they might seem.

Before entering the hallowed halls of this University of the Universe, all souls enter into a contract which states that, unless they attain their self prescribed, evolutionary goals, they will not leave. This has been done to prevent them from giving up and retreating without achieving their objectives. Nevertheless, in frustration and despair, many have found ways to give up and drop out, such as suicide, illness, addiction, insanity or even by becoming a monk or nun. In truth, there is no escape no matter what you do! That's why this line from the song "Hotel California" rings so true, "you can check out anytime you like but you can never leave." Whatever situation you try to escape from will resurface and confront you again, in this life or another. You may choose to be a victim and suffer the experiences, or masterfully overcome them no matter how complex, painful or heart wrenching they may seem. The key is to face the challenges with awareness, to unlock the wisdom within them and free yourself from their energetic influence. Conscious learning and growth require you to take responsibility for what you are experiencing and resolve issues at a deep inner level without blaming yourself or others. Then every experience will lead to accelerated maturity, self growth and spiritual evolution. Suffering and pain become superfluous and are replaced by pleasure and wisdom on this accelerated path to enlightenment.

No grand scheme for salvation can ever bring about a mass exodus from this world. Such ideas make for wonderful fairy tales and fantasies but are actually contrary to the fundamental purpose for which this Universe was created.

The second flaw: suffering.

From a physical and mental perspective, the world appears to be full of suffering. Death, disease, aging, hunger and loss are some of the numerous miseries that surround the human experience, waiting to strike at any time. The messiahs of religion, politics, economics, science, medicine and technology all focused their energies on alleviating human misery and at first they appeared to be making great progress but in time their amazing solutions proved to be fraught with even greater problems than the ones they had tried to solve. All of them succeeded in providing short term relief for a few, while inadvertently creating long term pain for the vast majority. If one half of the world became prosperous, the other half was starving; if transportation was made easy through cars, air pollution and accidents became deadly killers; if one terrible disease was cured another would spring up in it's place. Peace marches and the United Nations were unable to end war and, despite the advances in science, they were unable to free the world from the real hardships of unhappiness, lack, fear, poverty, disease and death. Religion brought peace to its congregation while fragmenting the world and breeding fanaticism.

Rohit: It feels natural to be compassionate and desire to alleviate the suffering of others. Whats wrong with compassion?

God: Compassion is wonderful when it empowers a person but it can be disempowering when it feeds into their sense of victimization. The world has been inundated with brilliant ideas that were supposed to eliminate suffering, yet no one has succeeded. This is because suffering is an internal phenomenon and cannot be eliminated through external means.

You are free to create and experience whatever you desire. The world is your playground. You are the creators of the heaven or hell you are experiencing. The challenges you are facing are exactly what your soul chose to work on in this life. The tougher the challenges your soul has presented you, the more evolved and capable you are to deal with them. The intense turmoil and chaos that you see today is indicative of the advanced learning experiences that you have collectively chosen. For the mind, it makes no sense why anyone would make such choices, but for the soul, all experience is rich and transformative. There is no wrong choice. As souls you are all indestructible. Every experience that you have will enrich you, empower you and ultimately bring you to the awareness of how incredible you truly are. In the final analysis, nothing can ever actually harm you. Suffering is the byproduct of your personal mythology. Heaven is within you, right here, right now!

Religion made people spiritually lazy, dependent and disempowered. The messiah or messenger of God was supposed to suffer for you, do all the work and take you to heaven. It was like having a guaranteed paycheck for the rest of your life along with heavenly retirement benefits. As a result, the world is full of unevolved fanatics chasing the latest ideology, technology, trend or savior, ready to work hard, give their lives and follow their leader to the edge of the proverbial rainbow.

You are the cause of all your pain and misery and only you can free your self. You can create heaven on Earth for yourself but no one else can do it for you. That is the bottom line. I know it doesn't sound very compassionate given your present outlook but, as I see it, true compassion is a process of empowering people to find the root cause of their problems and to develop the skill to resolve their issues from the inside out.

Instead of trying to alleviate suffering through externally based solutions, if humanity had focused on developing mental resilience, inner technologies and spiritual wisdom, perhaps there would have been no need for salvation through religious, political, industrial or technological revolutions. If people had been taught to operate their mind computer, decode their emotions and connect with their spiritual essence they would have freed themselves from suffering and lived blissful lives, irrespective of their challenges.

Saviors make people lazy, foolish and arrogant. When you realize that no one is coming to save you, you have no option but to wake up and take action to either save yourself or suffer the consequences.

The third flaw: the cure-all.

Irrespective of which path you take, the ultimate result of all forms of salvation is the same. To the extent that you believe in a particular thought or ideology you are likely to become closed to all other points of view. This is how you begin to lose clarity, objectivity and empathy, while at the same time becoming prone to assumptions, manipulation and blind faith. The more you think you know it all or that you have achieved, accomplished, succeeded or arrived, the more you are likely to experience a sense of superiority and even arrogance.

The messiahs and neo-messiahs achieved popularity because they made highly desirable goals easily attainable through automated processes such as joining a religion, buying the latest gadget or popping a pill. Promises of instant success produced lethargy and a deterioration of human potential. For example, dependence on doctors and medication made people lose all awareness of the body's ability to heal itself. Dependence on technology made people lose touch with the extraordinary capabilities of their minds, which can outperform the best man made gadgets. Dependence on religion resulted in minimizing personal growth and maximizing fanaticism.

The idea that someone or something can solve all of your problems is nothing but a glorious illusion. True spiritual growth has nothing to do with release from suffering, going to heaven or avoiding hell. There is no value in such escapism, neither will you earn brownie points for such measures. You chose to incarnate in physical form and come to this world. Why? Certainly not so that you could get out of here as quickly as possible. You don't go somewhere just to get out of there. This amazing, complex, beautiful, Universe wasn't created just so you could pray your way out of it and neither was it created to be a place of suffering. Pain is the experience you have when you don't follow the road signs, the instructions that your inner voice or intuition is trying to give you.

Thousands of years have passed and the all the saviors haven't been able to make the world a better place. In fact things have gone from bad to worse. Moreover, if the billions of people who embraced religion had actually been saved, they would have been in heaven making it an other hell and hardly anyone would have been left on Earth. That hasn't happened. The promise of instant salvation was like a post dated check written by someone who had no money in the bank. It was a great idea, a powerful intention and a great myth.

Rohit: Whats the way out? What do we need to do?

God: When you entered this physical universe, this three dimensional learning environment, you were given the body and mind as tools to navigate this world. You were supposed to explore how they function and enhance their capabilities so that they could support you in your ultimate life purpose: the expansion of consciousness. All your thoughts and emotions, actions and experiences, creations and realizations are data that is sent back to Source, causing consciousness to expand. Everything you do, think, feel, experience or create, expands consciousness. All of you are here for only one task - to expand consciousness. That is the whole point of creation, existence and life. The purpose of life is to expand consciousness, to evolve God and to unveil the magnificence of existence. You are all involved in this evolutionary process. The saint and the sinner, the hero and the tyrant, the abused and the abuser are all valuable aspects of the wheel of spiritual evolution. When you participate unconsciously, without full awareness of how to optimally use your mind, body and soul, your contribution becomes tedious and belabored at best. Yet everything you contribute is useful and all data meaningful. However, when you become conscious through the practice of meditation and spirituality, then your body, mind and soul become aligned with the intention for which you incarnated in the physical Universe. Your journey then becomes an exciting, blissful, adventure. This was the original path of the the mystics, the wizards, the witches and the yogis. They were having fun experimenting, exploring and creating inner technologies; that is, until religion came along and attempted to wipe them out.

The solution to life's challenges does not lie in some magical cure-all, or in going to some better place. What you are seeking lies within you. It has always been there, while you looked all over the world to find it. When you learn to operate the mind computer, one of the first things you learn is how to turn it off and the moment you do, you experience an alternate reality, a place of power, peace, joy and love within you. It was there all along. When you learn to bring this soul energy into your life then you begin to live from a place of clarity, ease and flow. The world is no longer feels like a fearful place, life is no longer a struggle for existence and things do not affect you as they formerly did. A resilience builds within you that allows you to weather the storms of life with greater peace, equanimity and balance. You are at home with yourself and the world.

The fourth flaw: scriptures.

Over the ages, humankind has been fascinated with the idea of God and has made countless attempts to define me. Yet most people, including the priests and preachers, know very little about the impersonal or personal aspects of God. Without any direct experience, they resort to outdated books that have been distorted, misinterpreted and bear little resemblance to the original teachings of the prophets or messiahs. These so-called, holy books are filled with parables, stories and concocted theories that lull your mind to sleep so that you do not think. These so called scriptures are supposed to be the "word of God" but were never spoken by me, say very little that is true about me and do not represent me in any way.

Scholars who have interpreted these scriptures claim to be presenting the only, true, authentic, version of the "word of God." Preachers with their rhetoric, wit and charisma dish out brilliantly crafted sermons and brainwash millions of people. Their holy books have been used to inflame passions, divide people, instigate hate, destruction and murder in the name of God. Why do they do it? For power, fame and money? To become the richest, most influential and powerful people on the planet?

I have never written any scripture. The messiahs and messengers of God never wrote anything. All scriptures are heresay and therefore heresy. They were compiled from bits and pieces of information about the messiahs and their teachings, that had been passed down over time.

These were then merged with stories and legends of the time and finally embellished with poetic language. The entire project was initiated, supported and funded by Monarchs who knew that there was no better way to control people than by making them obey the "word of God."

There is no authentic scripture. There is no scripture that truly represents me. At the same time, all of them contain fragments of truth which makes them very powerful. However, the words of wisdom are often so cleverly intertwined and mired in the web of falsehood that it is impossible for most people to separate the lies from the truth.

All scriptures say the same thing and yet they say nothing. If you believe in them blindly, follow them literally and argue with each, other quoting words and phrases to prove yourself right and others wrong, then you have understood nothing. You have read what you thought was God's word, developed a "holier than thou" attitude and understood nothing about God. As long as you think of me as the Lord, Judge and Controller of the Universe, you will take whatever has been written about me in the scriptures as the absolute truth. You will interpret their meaning, turn them into law, worship them, memorize them, debate your views and ultimately be willing to fight and kill for them. When the core concept of God is false, the outcome will always be flawed. Faith is the suicidal weapon with which you will destroy your common sense, corrupt your soul and retard your inner growth.

Many are angry with God because they believe that "He" is responsible for all the chaos and destruction the world has known. To pass the buck and make God responsible for all your problems is the perfect path to helplessness and victimhood. Whether you use this logic to reject God or reject logic to become a believer, either way they are contributing to the problem. To be truly responsible you must get to the heart of the matter and change things. This will happen when you put aside your books and beliefs and discover the truth through the direct experience of communion with your soul, Self and God. Scientific inquiry requires theory, experiment and conclusion. Let this book and others like it be your theory, perform the experiments on yourself, and be willing to let go of of any preconceived notions. Keep exploring and expanding, arrive at no conclusion, for the search for truth, is an end in itself. Stay open, believe nothing and you will awaken to the ultimate truth about yourself and God. As you live that truth and weave it into every aspect of your life, your world and everything around you will change, from the inside out.

The fifth flaw: faith.

Rohit: All humans want to believe in something. In fact life could appear really strange if we didn't believe in something or the other. Whats wrong with belief?

God: What you believe determines what you do. Look at the history of humankind and you will see, in man's actions, the chaos and destruction that beliefs have created over the centuries. All war, murder, rape, materialism, torture, terrorism and other distorted behaviors that you have seen humans do for thousands of years are the result of these misguided beliefs. Belief is the software of the mind computer. Once you know or believe something, you are unlikely to question it and thereafter be closed to any other possibilities. Knowledge and belief are the mind's way to streamline its operation and create a comfort zone for itself, regardless of the consequences. Whatever you think you know will make the mind complacent. The more you believe something to be true, the more rigid, arrogant and fanatical you will be.

Unlike religion, I ask you to believe nothing. I want you to first experience, feel, know, and then let go, unlearn and regularly restart from the point of not knowing anything. This requires humility, curiosity, openness, inquiry, receptivity, exploration and experimentation. You are invited to stretch your mind and remain open to all possibilities. You may, at times, need to momentarily speak as if you know or act as if your exploration is true. There is no harm in that. The idea is not to become indecisive, vague or confused. Expansion occurs when you unlearn everything that you have learnt. The absolute truths of one era are the absolute untruths of another. Everything is true and untrue simultaneously. In every truth lies an untruth and in every untruth lies a truth. The only thing that is real is the mystery, the unknown and the infinite realm of possibilities. To think that you know is an end point, the death of inquiry, curiosity and wisdom.

Spirituality is the science of unknowing, of returning to your original state of wonder, fascination and amazement. There is nothing easy or instant about spiritual growth. It takes smart work to change your thinking, transform your attitudes, break your resistance, heal your emotions and shake off erroneous beliefs and thoughts. Spiritual evolution is a personal journey that each one of you must take alone. Spirituality is personal and individual, it is not something for mass consumption. No teacher, messiah, scripture, religion or institution can ever help you evolve. Only you can do that for yourself.

The sixth flaw: preachers.

The preachers, priests and gurus were mostly rabble rousers. Their charade of piety and holiness, their oratory and charisma masked their lack of wisdom, humility and their disconnection from God. In order to attract followers they became like salesmen and lawyers, arguing the merits of their deeply held beliefs. They created lofty standards of right and wrong for their followers. Rarely would they practice what they preached. They hid their personal lives behind a veil of secrecy and surrounded themselves with bodyguards and secretaries who made sure that no one got too close to them. This isolation generated an illusion of piety, purity and holiness. It concealed their weaknesses, secret activities, investments, love affairs, sexual abuses and all other actions which ran contrary to their fabricated teachings and artificial standards of morality.

Their teachings were impossible to follow because they were unnatural and ungodly. They invariably fell prey to their own deep-rooted, unresolved issues and thrived on the innocence of followers who believed blindly, followed fanatically and chose to live in a fool's paradise. Neither the preachers nor the followers realized the trap they had walked into. The blind lead the blind and all of them fall into a ditch. Some of the more fortunate ones discovered the lies and left the religion, weakened, embittered and hopeless while others hung on for dear life, with their eyes closed.

Unless priests, preachers and gurus get honest with themselves, work on healing their own unresolved issues, let go of their false beliefs, surrender their egos, connect with their soul and listen to God's guidance from within, they will not be able to help anyone.

Preacher, save thy self!

The seventh flaw: sin.

Religion claims that you are the product of "original sin," that you are inherently sinful, flawed and unwanted. They claim that you have inherited the legacy of Adam and Eve, from which you cannot escape unless you accept the messiah and atone for your sins. Only then will you be saved from the eternal fires of hell and damnation. Each religion has taught its followers some version of this horror story. They have all been brainwashed with some notion of sin and the end result has been chaos. Fear hasn't worked. Fear cannot work.

Let the truth be known: the Lord thy God hath declared, for all time, past, present and future, that there is no such thing as sin, there are no sinners, there is no judgment day or hell and no one needs to be saved. You are all wonderful as you are. You are all worthy and deserving of everything you desire. God will never judge, punish or condemn you no matter what what you do. You are loved unconditionally, as you are, regardless of what anyone thinks.

All of you are completely free to think, feel, do whatever you desire and face the consequences. If, however, you act against the free will of another you will give rise to a karmic mirror that will cause you to experience what you caused in the other. This is not a punishment for your sins, it is an opportunity for you to step into the shoes of the one whom you harmed and hopefully develop empathy.

Your inner world generates your outer world. Your thoughts, beliefs and feelings give rise to your reality. You are the only one who can save yourself by taking responsibility to alter your thoughts, beliefs and choices.

Salvation is a mythical, fool's paradise. To save people from their sins is an act of futility. Unless people change from within, they will recreate their mind-generated hell wherever they go. Unless their consciousness changes, they will remain stuck in the same chaotic loop of the past, repeatedly attract similar situations and being miserable.

The true intent of redemption is to re-deem, re-declare or re-invent yourself. To declare that you are a spiritual being, a pure, beautiful, enlightened soul, abundantly worthy and deserving of all that you desire. You cannot be defined or limited by your thoughts, emotions, beliefs, body, religion, nationality or possessions. To redeem means to awaken and live an amazing life. By fearlessly claiming your spiritual identity and taking back power from your mind computer, you will be able to easily let go of traumas from the past along with fears for the future. You will connect with your spiritual power and begin to re-create life in alignment with your highest truth. You will become your own messiah and save your self.

Journal

CHAPTER 31

The Curse of Righteousness

God: Perhaps the most dramatic reason for the failure of the "Age of the Messiahs" was an unprecedented rise in righteousness and fanaticism. As the experiment of salvation progressed, the collective mind of humanity became obsessed with the thought that their truth, ideology, system or product was the best. The more inflexible, rigid and closed one's version of the truth, the more righteous and fanatical one is likely to become. The egoic mind thrives on thinking that it is right, better or superior. Righteousness, like a drug, intoxicates the ego, making it addicted to believing that it is right and all who disagree are wrong. Those who understood the power of righteous energy used it to manipulate, control and subjugate people. They bypassed the mind's logical processing and filtering system by asking people to jump directly from belief to truth without the need for proof or direct experience. Religion, money, politics, science, advertising, media and technology became the delivery mechanisms to exploit people and brainwash them.

Religion was the original and most successful proponent of

righteousness. By making God the ultimate authority and by manipulating his "commandments," the clergy discovered the ultimate way to control people and make them act without thinking. The words of God or the prophet were altered to justify mass murder, torture, rape etc. It was the ultimate hijacking of human consciousness!

That was until politicians, scientists and corporations got on the bandwagon and followed suit. They marketed their ideologies, their products and themselves as superior. They lulled people into working hard and devoting their lives to some idealistic vision. The followers, blinded by hope, could not see that the path they were on and the pot of gold they were being promised, would turn out to be nothing but a big hoax. A few would attain everything that they desired, while the masses would slave mindlessly, barely making ends meet. The unstoppable power of righteousness led to the unabashed desire for competition, conflict, exploitation and conquest. These tendencies had always existed, but as righteousness spread they gained validity and momentum. Gradually, one planet fragmented into many splinters based on nationality, religion, race, color and economic status. The delusional waves of righteousness spread everywhere, contaminating almost every aspect of human life. It infected believers and non believers, atheists and theists, the law abiding and the criminals, the young and the elderly, the lovers and the warriors.

Righteousness is based on the presumed belief in an incontrovertible, absolute truth. Religion codified its truth in the scriptures, politicians in the Constitution, judiciary in the law books, scientists in the axioms of mathematics and science. Volumes of books were written on every subject to attempt to define the laws that would control every aspect of human life.

The truth, along with its companions, righteousness and fundamentalism, found great appeal and spread like wildfire. The truth was supposed to set you free. It motivated people, gave them direction and spurred them into action with its testosterone driven, competitive, masculine energy. It gave people a way to go beyond their small self and act for the larger good of their society, community, country or religion. So blinding was this phenomenon that people were ready to go to war, engage in acts of terrorism and give up their lives to uphold, defend and spread it. The righteous believed that their truth was the truth, that they were good and justified, while those who did not believe, look or behave as they did, were potentially bad and untrustworthy. From these misconceptions arose waves of intolerance, quarrel, torture, killing and destruction that have plagued the Earth for thousands of years. This led to the Inquisitions, Crusades, the Holocaust, World Wars and the fundamentalist movements of present times. Mass murder, torture, rape, looting and destruction were all justified because a group of people had been convinced that they knew what was best everyone.

It had all originated from the fear that, without a deeply ingrained conception of truth, without something authoritative that told people what was right and wrong, they would go astray, commit crimes and do all kinds of inhuman and reprehensible acts. Unfortunately, this is exactly what the double edged sword of truth made them do! Like the pied piper of Hamelin the religious and neo messiahs led millions of people up their various paths of salvation and down to the abyss of death and destruction. They all had good intentions which worked for a while but in the long run it played havoc with the lives of their followers, spreading untold misery and anguish. Instead of freeing people from suffering as they had promised, they multiplied the distress of humanity by taking away the power and freedom of those who followed them, and destroying or victimizing those who did not.

Rohit: Life without laws, rules, morality, right and wrong, does seem scary if not downright insane to most people. How can one possibly live in this way, won't the very fabric of human society be torn to shreds? Will it not lead to chaos, anarchy and mindless destruction?

God: What you fear has already happened. It has happened because of righteousness, in spite of all the law books, religions, priests, police, government and armies. There is no one thing to blame, it is a disease that goes deep into the very nature of the human mind and it is there that you will find the root of all of your problems, along with the solutions.

In fact, there is no such thing as "THE truth." Every truth is a lie waiting to be exposed. Every lie has within it an element of the truth. Every preacher, lawyer, politician, and marketing person knows how to use this principle to twist the facts and prove their point. By the time they are done, lies appear to be truths and truths are no longer believed. The truth, instead of setting people free is thus often used to control, dominate and establish superiority. The search for truth is the ultimate trap for the human mind. What you think can be understood is often untrue and what you think cannot be understood, often holds within it the greater truth.

Any religion or ideology that attempts to tell people how to live, think and believe is only casting them into the straitjacket of righteousness and leading them up the garden path. Life is not fair or just. It just is what it is! Morality doesn't make people good, most of the time it breeds repression and perversion. Reality is the greatest illusion of all. Laws are for fools. Nothing is better than anything. No one is better than anyone. No one can save anyone or make the world a better place. The world is already perfect, you have always been perfect and perfection is always perfecting itself.

Rohit: Why did righteousness and fanaticism spread so universally?

God: Everyone wants to be right. This is because the egoic mind is righteous by nature. It presumes that its perception and conclusions are the truth. It also believes that its version of the truth is superior to that of others. It then attempts to prove or even impose its truth through argument, conflict, emotions or force. Finally, it wants to be validated and acknowledged for being superior. This primal survival mechanism, which Darwin referred to as the survival of the fittest, shows up in humans as the flourishing of the so called fittest through competitiveness and achievement, as well as the acquisition of wealth and power.

In small doses, the mind experiences righteousness as healthy self esteem, respect for others and responsibility. In larger doses, as the illusion of superiority increases, you may find yourself inclined towards arrogance, insensitivity and domination. To the extent that the mind is unable to feel superior in some way, it may begin to experience varying levels of mental ill health such as low self esteem, depression, victimhood etc. Please consider that all of the above examples are broad generalizations and there are many variations and exceptions.

The race towards the flourishing of the fittest was daunting and even devastating for most people. There was only so much room at the top. The egoic mind discovered an alternate path which could be observed, both in so called free societies and dictatorships, amongst the rich and poor, the religious and atheists. By surrendering personal power, individuality and self determination to an authority figure, ideology, system or dogma, the ego could easily meet its need to feel right and get validation. It felt safe, comfortable and included as part of a homogenous group.

Every group ideology that binds people together under a common truth, belief or identity inadvertently breeds an "us" which automatically gives rise to a "them." From this dichotomy comes an ego generated feeling of superiority or in some cases victimization. The egoic mind struggles to deal with its most primal fear - annihilation of itself. To alleviate this fear, people group together as families, communities, countries, companies, armies, religions etc. There is safety in numbers. The group clings together, shutting all others out, creating its own web and hierarchies, generating its own closed loop of beliefs, values and systems. Most groups are satisfied feeding off themselves, dealing only with their cult, tribe, community or nation. Some feed off others, they want to convert them, to make them conform to their ideals and if they don't they are perceived as a threat. They would rather kill them than be killed by them in some imaginary future. Fear dominates their thinking! Internally it takes over their mind and externally it strives to control their world. Wherever it goes, fear produces chaos, havoc and suffering. Within the mind it clouds your thinking and in your world it makes you do things you would never normally do.

In most groups, the unique self merges with the group consciousness and becomes increasingly identified, dependent and compliant with the groups perceptions, expectations and values. This often results in deterioration of critical thinking, discernment and empathy. Religion, society, schools and universities teach people everything except how to manage their mind or emotions, think outside the box or challenge conventional thinking. This is no accident. The conditioned or brainwashed mind is an easy target for manipulation. When the situation demands it, the individual can easily be incited to engage in acts of subtle or gross violence, towards the self or others, without guilt or fear of the consequences.

Collective righteousness invariably causes one group of people to feel justified in gaining supremacy over others. The ensuing religious, national, economic or racial disparity may have far reaching consequences such as an unequal distribution of power, wealth and resources. Monarchies and capitalism have proven this beyond a shadow of doubt. Communism and socialism have proven that the opposite does not work either. When everyone is forced to be the same, the enforcers, the army or government, invariably become greedy and incensed with power. They end up creating extreme power structures that inevitably crumble.

When one group of people has more, those who have been deprived will sooner or later rise up in rebellion, resistance and opposition. They will overthrow governments, kill innocent people and sacrifice their lives. True equality, sharing of resources, power and wealth cannot be achieved by such artificial systems. They require a revolution in consciousness, where one naturally wants to share, honor, love oneself and others.

In time, the principles of righteousness became universal. Ideals such as truth, fairness, justice, virtue, morality, piety, virginity, fidelity, honesty, goodness, decency, loyalty, trust and faith became deeply embedded in the human psyche and upheld by people all over the world. Did these ideals really serve anyone? Could anyone consistently live up to them? At what cost and for how long? Under what circumstances would they deviate? Did these ideals set you up for failure? Did they cause some people to become disillusioned and swing to the opposite extreme, becoming heartless criminals, soulless politicians or exploitative corporations? The reality is hard to face because, which ever way you look at it, whether you conform or rebel from these man made truths, either way you find yourself trapped.

The truth cannot be conceived by the mind, it must be felt and experienced in the heart and soul. The truth cannot be made into laws and rules for it is neither static nor universal. The truth is an ever changing kaleidoscope that can only be known in silence, felt in stillness and experienced in a state of wonder.

Journal

CHAPTER 32

The Rise and Fall of Fanaticism

Rohit: Ancient civilizations inspired everyone to strive for personal growth and enlightenment throughout their lives. In Earth based cultures everyone was taught reverence for nature and all creatures. In the Vedas, it is mentioned that children were trained in meditation and spiritual practice from the age of five. Adults actively sought inspiration and guidance from enlightened beings. They strived to live by ideals that brought inner peace as well as harmony to themselves, their family and society. As elders they detached from work, family and home and devoted themselves to spiritual practice. Religious fundamentalism has reached a frenzied pitch all over the world. The fundamentalists of various religions want to destroy each other. Is there a way out of this mess?

God: With the advent of organized religion, concepts such as salvation replaced the need for spiritual practice, meditation and self development. The prophet or messiah was supposed to take care of everything. A healthy dose of guilt was all one needed to confess and atone for ones sins. Guaranteed salvation made people spiritually lazy. They no longer needed to look within and improve themselves. Faith caused them to stop thinking, questioning, learning and growing. As their consciousness weakened, people became willing puppets in the hands of powerful rulers and religious institutions.

It was only with the advent of scientific thought and "the age of reason" in the 17th century, did an increasing number of people began to challenge the validity of religion and the monarchy. Unfortunately, what began as philosophical and scientific inquiry, rapidly turned into a rejection of everything metaphysical. Science focused its attention on empirical knowledge that could be observed and measured by the senses. All inquiry that did not fall into the narrow parameters of sensory perception was rejected as unscientific. In the 20th century, two major revolutions in physics began a gradual shift in the limitations of the classical scientific paradigm, they were the theory of relativity and quantum mechanics. This led to a deeper exploration into the role of energy and consciousness.

Rohit: It seems as though the past century has seen a massive resurgence of spirituality throughout the planet. It is as if the soul of humanity has been waking up to its inner power. With this awakening has come great upheaval. People all over the world have began rejecting the control exerted on them by social norms, businesses and governments. They have been rising up, protesting, toppling governments and institutions of power.

God: Peace marches, prayer vigils, non violent and violent protests, treaties, summits and the United Nations have only partially been able to alleviate the problems facing the planet. The problems of the world cannot be solved by such endeavors. The root cause, and the solution to the world's problems, lies within each of you. When you find peace within, there will be peace in your world, when your inner chaos dies down the world around you will become harmonious, when you truly love yourself without judgment or shame there will be love wherever you go.

As an example, lets take the rise of religious fundamentalism. The terrorists, as well as the armies that hunt them down, are all fanatics. Each side is absolutely convinced that their opinion is the truth and the others are wrong, deluded or brainwashed. Ultimately, the fault finder and the wrong doer, the tyrant and the victim trade places, doing to each other that which was done to them. The principle of action and reaction is the same for everyone. Anger begets anger, hate begets hate, violence begets violence and fanaticism begets fanaticism. The victims of one brand of terrorism give rise to another. Karmic reactions increase in intensity, expanding endlessly with each reaction spiral.

Fanaticism is not the prerogative of a particular group of people. It is a mindset, a way of thinking and perceiving the world. The mind and ego want you to believe that that the thoughts, perceptions and opinions they concoct are the truth, that you are right and those who disagree are wrong. The result is judgmental, righteous, intolerant, bigoted, racist, sexist, fanatical behavior. Whoever thinks they are right is a fanatic! That means almost everyone, depending on the extent of their affliction, is guilty of contributing to the rise of fanaticism.

Your collective consciousness has given birth to this new holocaust that now haunts your world. What you are seeing is a mirror reflection of your own rigid and fanatical thinking about how the world should be, what is right and wrong, good and evil. When you think you are right, by inference you assume that others who think or act differently are wrong. When you insult someone, criticize, fault find, backbite, judge or accuse another, you are being righteous. When you impose your truth on others, when you think you are right and make others wrong, they will inevitably react with anger and even hate.

The insanity of fanaticism feeds on its own hysteria, eating into the soul of the person and mercilessly exploiting and destroying everything around them. In trying to destroy the enemy outside you will find that you are destroying yourself inside. If, in your rage against terrorism you react and declare war on the terrorists, they will react and bring about even more destruction on you.

In the battle of righteousness there are no winners. Fanaticism cannot be destroyed, suppressed or ignored. The only outcome is suffering, hatred, violence and destruction. Will it ever stop? No. Not until fanaticism stops - both yours and theirs. Not until religion ends. Not until countries cease to exist. Not until people are trained to subdue their negative thinking, discrimination and narrow mindedness. Until then, in the name of heaven, you will create hell on Earth. As long as you try to appease the Gods of money, power and religion, the wars will only get worse and humanity will sink deeper into pain and negativity.

If it is not stopped right now, fanaticism will grow unlimitedly and turn this entire planet into a place where no one is safe, free or able to think for themselves. You are all extremely powerful beings. Your thoughts, emotions, beliefs, desires and actions generate powerful energies that alter the fabric of existence. You are significant, you matter and you can bring about massive change just by altering the way you think, feel and perceive the world, as well as the people around you.

The only way out is to understand the folly of your thinking and shift your consciousness in the direction of forgiveness, compassion and love. The destruction of fanaticism in the world begins with yourself. Notice the fanaticism, the rigidity, the righteousness, the superiority that you feel and the arrogance in your heart. Stop your mind when it tells you that you are right and another is wrong, when it judges, criticizes and condemns you or others. Disbelieve your thoughts. Challenge your negative beliefs. Purge your heart and mind from the scourge of fanaticism and you will set in motion the most powerful force for change. When you take responsibility for having created fanaticism you will also gain the power to end it.

Journal

CHAPTER 33

Religion, the Antithesis of God

Rohit: Why are you so against religion?

God: Religion is ungodly, unholy and untrue. Religion is the antithesis of God and the nemesis of human evolution. Religion is anti God, anti life, anti love, anti peace and anti joy. No matter which way you try to defend it, the bottom line is that it is based on falsehoods and, for all its tall claims, it has not worked. By guaranteeing salvation, religion has made people spiritually weak, dependent, powerless, lazy, blind, foolish, fearful, arrogant and fanatical.

All religions are mind made. This may be observed in their dualistic teachings that propagate notions such as right and wrong, good and evil, should and should not. The mind thinks in dualistic terms, while spirit or God is by nature a non dual, all inclusive and unifying force. Religion relies on blind faith and belief, while zealously defending its ideologies from non believers. The distorted teachings of religion simulate the egoic mind. They offer little of value for the wellbeing of humanity or the evolution of consciousness.

Karl Marx said, "religion is the sigh of the oppressed creature, the heart of a heartless world, just as it is the spirit of a spiritless situation. It is the opium of the people." In my opinion he underestimated the power of religion and failed to see how insidious and horrific it truly is. If religion had only drugged people with opium it would have been harmless. Instead, it has turned innocent people into murderers and made devils out of wannabe saints. Religion distorted the wise and profound teachings of evolved souls in order to serve its vested interests. Religion turned God into a puppet and made him dance to its discordant tunes. It made God a genie who would answer people's prayers and grant their wishes. That was the carrot that was dangled in order to hook everyone. Then came the evil, judgmental, wrathful nature of God. That was the stick they used to divide and rule humanity. Religious preachers filled people with guilt, repression and self-loathing and at the same time, spread hate, prejudice and discrimination against non believers. Religion has been its own greatest enemy and has brought about its own inevitable demise. It has been the cause of the downfall of humanity into materialism, chaos and anarchy. It has failed to make people love God or each other and it has effectively turned millions of people away from God.

I know this is a bitter pill to swallow. Millions who follow religion will rise in anger and denounce what I am saying as sacrilegious. In truth it is their bastardized version of God that is the ultimate sacrilege, blasphemy and heresy. The guilty believers shall arrogantly proclaim their righteousness and, with great indignation, attempt to thwart all attempts to expose their falsehood. They would not want to know the truth about God, even if God were to stand before them and speak to them personally. Religion has filled them with false hopes and empty promises. Now they sit comfortably ensconced in the superiority of their

Religion, the Antithesis of God | 243

beliefs and the assurance of their salvation. Why would they let anyone rock the boat? I agree, I did not want to disturb them either. I prefer to give freedom, let each person discover for him or her self where the path leads, learn from their experiences and, in time, decide what worked and what did not.

However, the problem has got out of hand. The ideal of salvation has failed and in its place has emerged the egoic philosophy of us versus them, my religion is better than yours, my way is the only way and all non believers must be destroyed. When you combine this thinking with the increasing gap between the wealthy and poor nations, the intense frustrations of the underprivileged and the easy availability of weapons of mass destruction, you end up with a highly combustible situation. Religion has become the vehicle of choice for fanatics to unleash their anger on the rich and powerful who have exploited them.

What is bizarre about this entire situation is that God is not on anyone's side. God is busy playing golf, making love, romancing life, celebrating existence and inviting you to join in. This does not mean that God is indifferent to your problems. The truth is that God is not going to keep cleaning up your mess. I am here to motivate you to take action. God is not your handy man who will fix everything you break. To do so would be to disempower humanity and repeatedly recreate the chaos. The world changes when you change: when you understand the cause, take responsibility, then alter your thoughts, beliefs and actions. The chaos in the world begins and ends with you... each of you!

Journal

CHAPTER 34

The Way Out

Rohit: It all sounds quite messed up. What can we do?

God: I have stepped in to bring clarity, dispel the myths and hopefully accelerate a shift towards peace and sanity. I am the chief accused (or revered) in this drama and it has become imperative for me to come forward and expose the machinations of the well intentioned powers that be. I cannot stand by any longer and let this fiasco carry on. I must speak now, because to keep silent any longer will only lead to unimaginable chaos and destruction at a scale far greater than anything you have witnessed so far. I must speak the cold, hard, unpalatable truth and it must be said emphatically and repeatedly until it sinks into your consciousness. The implications of this truth run deep and it will take a lot of work to expose the fallacies of religion, undo the damage it has done and finally reveal my true self to you. More than anything, my desire is to empower you with awareness and choice. Ultimately, you always have choice. This is your life and your planet and you are free to do with it whatever you desire.

The first step toward lasting change is internal and not external. Many have tried the path of external change and failed. Shortcuts and quick fixes have often made things go from bad to worse. Change your mind, open your heart and when your consciousness changes, the world will change. When you love the Earth, the plants, the animals and humans, then life will change. The dangers facing humanity will be averted. Alternately, you may sit back, do nothing, enjoy the ride and let nature take her course. To not act is also an action. Whatever you choose will be perfect.

The next step lies in changing your religious, political and economic concepts. You need to start from scratch. The existing systems of capitalism, communism, socialism, monarchy, democracy or dictatorship have worked for a few at the expense of the majority. It is time for everyone on the planet to have all that they need to live a decent life. For this to happen you must unite as one planet, undivided by religion, country, race, color or status. You must co-create one world, one currency, one economic structure along with equitable distribution of wealth and resources. This does not mean communism, marxism or socialism. It means that every individual on the planet must have equal earning potential as well as opportunities for education, work, food, health, safety, freedom and well being.

The capitalistic exploitation of planet Earth, its resources and its inhabitants in the name of economic progress must be stopped. The attempts to fight religious fanaticism through war-mongering and the spread of hatred must be stopped. Laws designed to curb freedom of speech, monitor and manipulate people must be scrapped at once.

Simplify your laws around one principle: free will. Allow people to be free to do as they wish as long as they do not forcibly act against the free will of any individual or community.

Cultivate in everyone a respect for the planet, which is your home, and without which all of your efforts are a waste of time. Move people away from cities and back to the land so that they may feel connected to the Earth.

The work must now begin in full earnest. All of you must get involved or the probability of the destruction of this planet and its inhabitants will increase exponentially over time. The signs are all around you, yet very few are willing to do whatever it takes to end the madness. Most of you are still sitting on the sidelines in denial, shell shocked and appalled, but without any clear vision on how to proceed.

Only time will tell if the turmoil generated by the egoic mind has caused more evolution or devastation. Up until this point humans have been riding the many waves of egocentricity, totally unconscious of its power to distort and destroy. In making you aware of its pernicious effects I hope that you will train yourself and those around you to live more consciously, peacefully and soulfully.

If you want to see a re-evolution of consciousness and a return from darkness into light, you need to set aside your differences, unite and collaborate. The more people that dedicate themselves to this task, the faster it will come about. Light workers, healers, therapists, spiritual guides and motivators must find common ground and work together. You may meditate, sing, dance, eat, celebrate, be there for each other, hold each other and spread love everywhere. This is your world. You are its creators and destroyers, its Goddesses and Gods. The planet is in your hands and only you can save it. I am here to support and guide you so that we may bring peace and love to the world, restoring Earth to her pristine glory.

To all of you that believe in me, have faith in me or think that you know me, I have one request. Please put aside all that you know. Be open and curious. Start from the beginning. In not knowing you will find me and in knowing you will lose me. Every one of you is extremely precious to me. I miss all of you. Let us reconnect and build a loving relationship. Allow me to reveal myself to you, to love you, to adore you, to cherish you and embrace the beautiful being that you are.

Journal

The Age of Awakening

CHAPTER 35

The Human Dinosaur

God: The Age of the Messiahs, the grand drama that held humans in its grip for thousands of years, is ending. The experiment is complete. The spell of illusion that has plagued the world for thousands of years has been broken, although the ripple effects it has set into motion will continue for a while. Chaos, destruction, war and killing will haunt the world for a few more years but ultimately it will wind down and come to a grinding halt.

Millions of souls across the Universe long to end the chaos, misery, destruction and suffering on Earth. They ardently desire to usher in a golden age of love, peace, joy enlightenment and empowerment, that I will refer to as the Age of Awakening. Humans will either change their ways and evolve their consciousness or become extinct like the dinosaur. This new era will come to pass at any cost. Nothing can stop it from happening.

The time has come for humanity to wake up from the dream of salvation. No one can ever save you, no science or technology, no amount of riches or fame will ever free you from suffering or give you what you truly desire. The time has come to turn inwards and discover the beauty, the enchantment and the power of your inner world. To discover the truth about who you are and why you are here. Live as a fearless, free spirit, filled with causeless joy and endless love, vibrantly alive and living life to the fullest. The Age of the Messiahs and all the suffering on this planet will then dissolve back into the field of infinite possibilities, from where it had once arisen, ending humanity's dramatic tryst with salvation, fanaticism and exploitation.

Rohit: If God is all things light and dark, then is it possible that, in some corner of creation, there might be a judgmental, wrathful God?

God: Yes and no. The God of religion was a mass produced thought virus designed to create massive chaos, thereby challenging humans to either accelerate their search for the truth or self destruct. A virus pretends to be real but, as soon as you click on it, it invades your computer causing massive harm. To say that a virus does not exist would be erroneous. It's not what it appears to be. That's all. The judgmental, wrathful God is merely an apparition, a ghost, a figment of the imagination that has haunted humanity. Although its effects are real and the suffering it has caused is astounding, it is in fact non existent.

While it was amusing for me to see myself cast into the outrageous possibility of being an autocratic monster, there comes a time when the play acting goes too far and the price for the games of a few, causes intense suffering for many. It is time to bring you back to the truth, to reinstate my original self, to reveal my eternal loving nature, so that you may know me as I am.

Journal

CHAPTER 36

The Illusion of Virtual Sensory Reality

God: All that you can imagine exists and simultaneously does not exist. All that appears real is in fact illusory and what appears illusory is often real. All that is, is not and all that is not, also is! Science has proven that 99.9% of all matter, if examined under electron microscopes, is in fact air. Everything you own, all that you desire, whatever you see, touch, hear, taste and feel is but an illusion. Everything is energy vibrating to create the illusion of reality, a façade masking the all pervasive nothingness which is the true nature of the universe. Everything is nothing and nothingness is the essence of everything. The entire Universe comes from nothingness and at some point dissolves back into it. Only to be manifest and unmanifest, to appear and disappear, again and again, as endless forms in the cosmic dance of creation.

In its pure form, existence is an energy field that is intelligent, wise, peaceful, loving and joyous. What you call reality is in fact virtual reality. The world and all that you perceive is a grand illusion, a waking dream, a three dimensional movie. As long as you believe in the illusion it will feel real, seem solid and it will have the power to hurt and control you.

On the other hand, imagination appears to be unreal, yet produces feelings that are as tangible as those produced by so called reality. Imagination impregnates thought, generates emotion and thrusts its seed into the fertile breeding ground of creation, existence and destruction. The dance of courtship between imagination, thought and emotion, gives birth to the virtual sensory reality that you experience. Just like imagination gives birth to reality, so does the experience of reality cause you to imagine and keep creating newer realities. Thus, imagination and reality walk hand in hand, creating each other, feeding off each other, manifesting illusions unlimitedly.

Reality is illusion and illusion is reality. They are one and the same. As long as it exists in someone's mind, imagination or delusion, as long as that person believes something, it will be experienced as real! At least for that moment, for that person, it will appear real and, through that person, its effects will be felt by all those who come in contact with him/her. For example a soldier who sees innocent citizens of another country as enemies may kill them even though the enmity he feels is real only to him and may not be in those whom he is killing. Yet once he has killed them, their loved ones are likely to be outraged and infected with the same feeling of enmity that was originally experienced by the soldier. The illusion has been passed on and will keep on breeding, endlessly.

All that appears to be true is ultimately false and, at times, that which seems untrue might conceal the greatest truth. In the unlimitedness of the Universe, in the infinity of God, all possibilities are always present. Existence is a collection of infinite shadow forms, clouds that take form in your senses and your imagination. In clouds or even in abstract art, once you have seen a particular form, its difficult to see something else. Your mind gets attached to its perception, unless you train it to hold multiple simultaneous possibilities, without accepting any as real or true.

The challenge is to see through the illusion, to look past the forms, circumstances and events, to see the delightful play of energy in everything that occurs. This will allow you to play with life rather than let it play with you. When your mind names a thing, believes in its existence and reacts to its presence, it is drawn into its self-created virtual sensory reality. You will find yourself getting drawn into situations, interacting with what your mind has created and becoming a puppet in its hands. Alternately, you may choose to be an observer, a witness, sitting back, enjoying the show, feeling, laughing and crying in the moment, yet able to step back and return to your inner world of peace and joy.

Seriousness turns the shadow-like events of life into hardened, earth shattering reality and playfulness turns even the most tragic circumstances into soft, ephemeral illusions. The more seriously you take your life, the more wrapped up you are in its stories and events, the greater the mind's power will be over you. It is only when you step back and learn to play the game of life with conscious awareness that none of this is real, that none of the situations are what they seem to be, then will you begin to truly enjoy every experience. If life is not fun at every step, then you are not living. If you are tense, stressed, anxious, worried or fearful, know that you are lost in the wilderness of a mentally concocted, illusory, virtual reality.

Rohit: If what you are saying has been said before, if the truth is timeless and eternal, if you are already speaking with everyone, if everything is going to be alright in the end then what is the need for writing this book?

God: Let us move from linear thinking to paradoxical thinking. Linear thinking is powerful because it is focused like a laser beam. The disadvantage is that singular perception creates tunnel vision, limitations and rigidity. Paradoxical thinking is expansive. It is the birds eye view that allows you to see multiple possibilities simultaneously. All realities are manifested thought bubbles from the Universal Energy Field of infinite possibilities. All truths are mind made. There is nothing absolute, real or lasting about anything manifest or unmanifest. Things exist, only because you believe in them. The moment you change your thinking, reality bends and the Universe folds, adapting to your perception, changing your world.

Journal

CHAPTER 37

The Ever Changing Word of God

Rohit: How about these ideas you speak to me now, are they also unreal and changing or is the word of God absolute and timeless?

God: Spiritual wisdom is eternal and timeless. At the same time it is constantly changing, altering and transforming itself. It is never absolute, rigid or static. Nothing is new in the Universe yet everything is constantly renewing, evolving and amazing itself. God is eternally reinventing, experimenting, exploring and creating new possibilities to expand the frontiers of consciousness.

Truth exists, but only for a moment, for an individual, in a given situation. At the same time the opposite is also true. This and its opposite are simultaneously true. Each moment is a truth bubble unto itself, round and perfect, complete and whole until the next moment when it bursts and is gone forever. Millions of such bubbles emerge simultaneously. Millions of eternal moments dissolve instantly. They are absolutely true for the moment and then they disappear into the vast nothingness.

Only in nothingness is the true nature of life revealed. In a state of no thought, the veil lifts and you are transported into an alternate vision of reality. A timeless, causeless, limitless vibrational space that is the true nature of all that is. You begin to see things as they are because, in that moment, you stepped off the treadmill, snapped out of the matrix and freed yourself from the illusion. Life changes forever when you see things as they are, when you step out of the clutches of your mind and awaken to the presence of your soul. Through the window of your soul you begin to see, hear, feel and experience God everywhere.

In this state of no thought, of no mind, I am able to connect and speak to you. I use thoughts, words, images, feelings, sounds, dreams and every form of communication possible to reach out to you. I tap into your life experiences and all that you know in order to relate to you. I inspire you to create great things and use your talents to benefit yourself and others. It matters little if you believe in me. I am not dependent on your belief systems. I exist whether you believe in me or not. For me, you are all my family, my loved ones, and I care about all of you equally. Most of you are unaware of my presence and the vital role I play in your lives. That is why I am communicating through books like this, so that our connection may transition from unconscious to conscious. When that happens, you will come alive in ways you never imagined possible.

Each individual's experience is unique. Each soul is on a unique journey. What is true for you may not be true for another. This is why, my words of guidance are customized to suit each of you and adapt to you as you grow and evolve. What is true today may not be true tomorrow. What works for you in the present may no longer hold true as you evolve. Times change, people change and the "word of God" is not static and frozen in time. In every moment, each of you are unique and different. So naturally, my messages are bound to change as you change and grow as you grow. They are a living, breathing, vital, powerful source of communication that needs to be customized, moment to moment, for each one of you.

Each one of you can tune in and listen to your own soulful whispers, your own inner voice and your own personalized message from me. You can write your own scripture, be your own savior or messiah and take responsibility for your own spiritual evolution. Only when you try out what I have told you from within and experience it in your own life, will it be true for you. Only then will you easily and rapidly move to higher levels of realization and consciousness.

Many of you are now sufficiently open-minded, evolved and ready to hear what I have to say. I feel that I can speak freely, with a frankness and candor that will open your eyes and bring all of us closer together. If you read my words with an open mind, they will download into you and reveal the power you have within yourself to live this wisdom effortlessly. You will certainly need help and I am here for you. I have waited millions of years for you to turn to me so that we may walk together, discover the essence of your soul, its unique gifts and amazing qualities.

At the same time, my words may shake up many of the long held beliefs and ideologies that the traditions of religion, society, culture and science have programmed into your psyche. These deeply ingrained beliefs have been taken for granted and rarely questioned. They are the cause of the misery, suffering and destruction that all of you have been experiencing. Instead of believing or disbelieving me, you may want to go within and feel if my words resonate at your core and whether or not they are in alignment with the deepest truth about who you are.

As long as you read, memorize, preach and argue over verses from scripture; as long as you depend on someone else to save, deliver liberate or take you to God; as long as you depend on anything or anyone other than yourself, you will be spiritually weak and make little to no progress. You will not experience your fullest spiritual potential or self actualization because you will have given your power and your trust to something or someone outside of yourself. Whoever or whatever you depend on will ultimately become your crutch, your stumbling block and your greatest obstacle to spiritual growth.

There are no free rides, there is no instant salvation and no one can uplift or save you. The messiah, the mantras and rituals that take away all your sins are an eye wash, a hoax, a fool's paradise created to take away your freedom, intelligence and power, while lulling you into obedience and servitude. They may give you momentary peace, comfort and help you to feel better but real spiritual growth takes responsibility, intelligence and perseverance. It's personal, individual, tangible and practical. Once you take the mythology and sentimentality out of your beliefs, you will experience salvation from your mind and all your troubles, right here and now.

You are not here to prove your worthiness, nor to earn your passage to heaven, nor to accumulate wealth, power or fame, nor to leave behind a legacy for the world or your children.

You are here to die! For one who has taken birth the only thing that is guaranteed is death. If you want to learn how to live fully, experience the heights of human potential or self actualization, you must first embrace death. Live as if you are already dead. Dead people are not afraid of dying, they do not accumulate things or try to impress others with their accomplishments. The death I am speaking about is not the death of the body or mind. It is a profound shift away from identification with the egoic mind and into the expanded awareness of your true essence, your true self, your soul. The world you see around you is a fools paradise created by those who are in denial of their own mortality. When you deeply embrace death you will discover that the purpose of life is life itself! You are here to die to all that is unreal and discover that which is real. You are here to discover yourself and God. This is the meaning of true spiritual evolution and growth.

For this, you do not need to read more books, attend more workshops, learn new techniques or seek great teachers. True evolution occurs when you silence your mind, open your senses and become present to the presence of God within everything and everyone around you. As you do this you will experience the true nature of reality which is peace, bliss, love, joy and ecstasy. I invite you to a world of heightened pleasure, exquisite enjoyment, and utter delight. I invite you to live as a soul in this world; I invite you all to live soulfully!

Journal

CHAPTER 38

The Path of the Mystics

God: The core of every evolved soul's teaching and the basis of all religions, scriptures and wisdom has always been the same. If you had been able to grasp and truly understand the essence of their teaching, there would have been no no separateness, no religious wars and no fanaticism. The symptoms and the resultant actions are proof that you have not understood them. What you have interpreted is so far removed from the truth, so distorted and convoluted that it makes me shudder to even think about what has happened.

If there was any truth in the religious perception of God, I would have been the first atheist. The atheist is as much a lover of God as the saint. Atheists are intelligent people who have seen through the contradictory teachings of religion and rejected their ridiculous God. They have not allowed manipulative, power hungry, religious zealots to pull the wool over their eyes. Without even realizing it, they have been saving themselves for the real thing. I admire their courage and intelligence. I agree with them but, unfortunately, they have created another religion.

They have "thrown the baby out with the bathwater" by rejecting God. Acceptance and rejection are both opposite sides of the same coin, both are mentally fabricated polarities that accept one perception while rejecting another. A science that operates within the limited parameters of sensory perception and logic is likely to create another belief system or religion. Real progress requires a scientific inquiry that considers all possibilities, explores all avenues and integrates all dimensions. When believers and non believers, fanatics and atheists, priests and scientists all exhibit similar, narrow minded, delusional thinking the outcome is likely to be chaotic and disastrous.

On the other hand there were mystics from every faith, born all over the world, like Christ, Buddha, Mohammed, Ali, Bulleshah, Rumi, Meera, Chaitanya and Osho to name a few. They followed no religion, they were free thinkers and mavericks who created unique pathways to God. They dared to challenge the religious orthodoxy and beliefs, of their time. In the desert, the forest, under trees, in caves, palaces and cities, they dived into the stillness of their soul and experienced God. They discovered the secret that religion had tried to conceal for centuries - the ecstatic, intoxicating and loving experience of a direct connection with God. They meditated, spoke, wrote, sang, danced and shared the ecstasy that they had found within. The fact that they were misunderstood and their teachings distorted, in no way diminishes their contribution.

True mystics and wizards are those who see through reality, circumstances, beliefs and truths with a kind of x-ray vision. They hold on to no thing, no one, no ideology and no belief system. They see God everywhere and are fascinated by everything. They rip apart all beliefs, tear down myths and break down illusions. They explore possible realities and truths, neither accepting nor rejecting any of them. They playfully innovate and create with childlike innocence.

Religious leaders could not tolerate the idea that someone could have a direct connection to God. If people believed this was possible then no one would come to their grand institutions to pray, be absolved of their sins or surrender their wealth. They labelled the mystics as mad, evil, witches or heretics. They humiliated, jailed, tortured and killed them in horrific ways. The mystics surrendered to God and felt no pain. Instead they felt compassion and a deep sadness at the plight of their fellow humans, who had turned from God in the name of God.

Times have changed. Most of the world is not as intolerant as it once used to be. I invite all of you to the path of the mystics. I long to reconnect with you and embrace you. Let us walk together, dance through life, celebrate existence and enjoy the beauty of this wonderful world.

The conditions are ripe to reach out to millions of people all over the world without much effort and spread this message of love and hope everywhere. Democracy has brought about freedom of speech and the internet has connected everyone. The time has come for everything to change. Let us all work together, especially those of you who have already begun the journey towards God. No matter what path you are on, I humbly request all of you to join hands and come together. It doesn't matter what you believe or which religion you follow. Let go of your differences and unite all religions, all beliefs and all people throughout the world as one family.

Do you really think that the God of all creation would favor one religion over another? Do you honestly believe that one teacher, guru, messiah or scripture is better than another? Of course not! It is sheer vanity, pride and arrogance to think that "mine is better than yours." How can it be? God is God! No true concept, understanding or description of God can ever be better that any other. Any teaching that unites people, honors creation, celebrates life and brings you even one step closer to God can never be wrong or bad. There is no right way, no truth or path that is correct for all. Wherever you are is right for you, whatever you think is perfect for you and whatever you believe is what you need for now. I am not asking you to change your path or your religion, all I ask is for you to separate the wheat from the chaff, the wisdom from the lies and experience the fruits of true spiritual evolution and enlightenment. If you cannot do that, at least just turn within, silence your mind through meditation and allow me to guide you.

Journal

CHAPTER 39

Communion With God

Rohit: You had said that, as the CEO of the Universe, God doesn't play an active role in the day-to-day affairs of this world. The Demigods manage everything and inspire people with new concepts and ideas. Now you say that you are communicating with all of us.

God: I'm glad you pointed that out. As I stated earlier, this, its opposite and much more are simultaneously true. There are numerous ways that I reach out to you, support you and remain connected with you:

(1) The Universal Internet (UI): As I had mentioned earlier, every experience, emotion and realization gained by any soul on any planet in the physical Universe is data that is fed back to an aspect of the Univeral Energy Field (UEF) that I earlier referred to as the Universal Internet (UI). To make the connection between these two terms very clear, the UEF is

like the world, it is everywhere, and the UI is like the internet which consists of a network of servers with millions of computers connected to them. Each of you is like a computer connected to the UI The data of all your experiences good or bad, ordinary or extraordinary, are equally valid, meaningful and valuable. No experience is better or worse. It is only data about the choices you made, the realities you created, the situations you attracted, the consequences and reactions that occurred are all collected through the Universal Internet. Through this continuous stream of data from infinite souls spread out through the vastness of outer space, the Universal Internet expands, consciousness evolves, expands and matures. In time, future generations are impregnated with updated versions of mental software, ready to take on new challenges and evolve consciousness to the next level.

The Universal Internet is the ever expanding and evolving wisdom of God. Just as your experiences shape and transform you, just as the inputs from millions of computers across the world shapes the internet, in much the same way, the collective inputs from infinite beings throughout creation expands and evolves the UI. In this way, you are all involved in the creation, evolution and expansion of God. This is why I said that God is not static, finite or absolute. God is constantly expanding, changing and evolving. As God evolves you evolve and as you evolve God evolves. Everything you do enhances and transforms God.

As God is, so are each of you. You are particles of God, droplets from the fountainhead, raindrops from the infinite sky, beams of light from the endless sun. God individuated as unique, infinitesimal, micro-gods, each living in their personal self made micro-universe. God experiences pleasure and suffering through you. You are a mirror through which God experiences itself.

Many humans have learnt how to download ideas, visions, creations and insights from the Universal Internet. These are received through the inner voice, which acts as a portal that receives insights in the form of voice, images, video, emotions and sensations from the UI. Most of those who are receptive are unaware of the source of their inspiration. They have stumbled on a process where inspired words, melodies, images or ideas just pop into their minds under certain conditions. This may happen when they are meditating, walking, relaxing or doing nothing. In that moment, when the mind is empty or still, they may experience intense clarity, insight or a shift in perspective. Many who have tapped into the UI have been hailed as geniuses for their original and brilliant thinking. They have become rich and famous beyond their wildest dreams.

The UI is a field of ever expanding knowledge, wisdom and creative possibilities. It is available to anyone willing to suspend judgment, be open and receptive. The more silent and still your mind is, the clearer the connection will be. The more you trust your inner voice and express it through writing, painting, music, innovation etc., the more powerful your creations will be. The more you act on the inner guidance, the more it will raise your consciousness, your abilities and the depth of your wisdom.

My intention is for all of you to avail of this incredible feature of human existence. The Universal Internet has unlimited bandwidth, there are no roaming charges, there is no need for any device such as a cellphone, tablet or computer. It is a natural technology that is available throughout the Universe at no extra cost. It will change your life, uplift your consciousness and metamorphose your world.

Rohit: How do I know if it is my inner voice or just the voices in my head?

God: Wisdom, insights and creations that come from the UI have a unique flavor. They are light, uplifting, energizing, expansive and inspiring. Thoughts that you process through your mind tend to leave you feeling just the opposite, heavy, tired or drained. You access the UI when your mind is quiet and silent. Thinking blocks your access, anxiety, worry or stress block access tot he UI.

Rohit: I like to say that my best thoughts come to me when I am not thinking.

God: That is what I mean. Through the inner voice I have inspired creative people, scientists and inventors. by inserting pearls of wisdom into music, art, science, literature and cinema so that you may have a glimpse of who you are and who I am. Through this inner voice I have attempted to guide every spiritual teacher and have seen their teachings distorted. Now, I am reaching out to all of you, eager to connect with you, speak to you and love you.

(2) Non Physical Guides: There is an entire non-physical world, filled with light and dark energies and entities, all around you. The demigods manage the operational functions of the Universe but they are not alone. Millions of highly evolved souls in non-physical form have volunteered to guide and support all of you through your human journey. They have been called spirit guides or angels.

Rohit: Do they have wings?

God: No! When they make themselves visible to the human eye, an optical illusion of wings is created due to the energy field surrounding them. This has been thought of as a useful way to distinguish themselves from ghosts or negative energies. Non-physical beings can travel instantly, at the speed of thought, anywhere in the Universe. They do not need primitive wings to travel across space where, without air, wings would be rendered useless.

Some of them have never been in human form, while others incarnated to experience the challenges of having a body, mind and emotions. This has helped them to develop empathy, skills and techniques that allow them to relate to the human condition. They now work on the subtle and astral planes supporting each of you, helping you fulfill your intentions and holding your hand as you go through your life journey. Each of them has taken on the care of many souls and can be with them simultaneously as needed. They are with you right now, invisibly connected at all times, working subtly in the background, attempting to reach out and guide you whenever you allow them. They speak to you through your inner voice, arrange situations and bring people into your life that will best support you on your path. They assist you in experiencing all that you believe, desire, think and create. They communicate with you whenever you are open and listening. They cannot help you as long as you are thinking, analyzing or in any way enmeshed in intricate web of your mind. Their purpose is not to answer your prayers by waving some magic wand. Instead, they attempt to guide, support and assist you in fulfilling your desires and solving your problems. What they desire most is the opportunity to support you in fulfilling your life purpose and enhancing your spiritual evolution.

They are fully surrendered to my will, my intention and my desire. I am deeply indebted to them for this wonderful, selfless service to humankind. They are deeply grateful when you collaborate with them in their compassionate, loving service to humanity. When you leave this body, you too may join them as a non-physical being if that inspires you.

Rohit: Earlier you said that you speak to us through the inner voice and now you say that spirit guides and angels do this work. Which is true?

God: Both are true. For the most part I have delegated everything to them. They act on my behalf. I personally step in when someone reaches out to talk with me, love me, when there is true, unmotivated, unconditional love.

(3) Earthly Messengers: through the ages I tried many ways to reach out and communicate with all of you. In recent times I have been flooding the world with highly evolved souls who are reaching out with their messages of love, peace and inspiration. They are all around you as children, friends, lovers, musicians, writers, artists, film-makers, television show hosts, healers and people you encounter. Many of them are free-spirited individuals, who live to serve others and make the world a better place. They reach out to you, share their wisdom, offer their support, guidance and love. You will notice that many of them are free from dogma, rules and institutions. They follow their inner guidance and use their talents

to inspire others. They live, work, enjoy life, make mistakes and struggle, just like everyone else. What sets them apart is their ability to constantly learn, evolve and grow, to remain humble, unpretentious and happy in most circumstances. They share one common purpose and that is to raise the consciousness of people all over the world. Their deepest desire is to bring peace and harmony so that everyone may enjoy the abundant gifts and opportunities that this wonderful planet has to offer.

Their words will ring true, touch you at the core, make you feel alive, free you from guilt and fear, bring out the best in you, help you heal and connect with your soul. They will generally not seek to make you dependent on them, follow them or look up to them. They must not be made into a guru or a God, for that will destroy them. Let them share with you what they have realized. Honor and thank them but do not put them on a pedestal. They are as human as you, entangled within the web of their own creations, struggling with their own minds and desires. Know that you too can be as they are, because all of you possess the same soulful qualities.

(4) Communion With God: I am by your side always, in the core of your being, in the depths of your essence, embracing your soul and loving you unconditionally. I am personally connected with each of you through your inner voice. You are a part of me and a part of me is always with you. We are always connected just as you are always connected with your friends and loved ones through instant messengers, Twitter and Facebook.

I witness, experience and feel everything that you are going through but remain a silent observer. I honor your free will and trust that whatever you choose to do will be the best for you. I rarely intervene in your life choices. I am not available to solve problems or fulfill desires. When things don't work out the way you want, when you desire more or when you feel troubled, I have an army of helpers available to support you with all your worldly issues. All desires, queries, prayers and pleas are taken care of by them. I am not available to be bribed or used for any gain or motive. The exception is when you reach out to me with humility, surrender and pure love. The call of your soul's longing brings me rushing to the door of your heart, ready to reciprocate your love and care for you in any way I can. I have been waiting for this moment when you will turn to me with your heart filled with unconditional love, unmotivated intention and unhesitant surrender. I am always ready to reconnect, reunite and revive our loving relationship. I am always ready to hold you in my loving arms and fill you with my presence. I am always ready to deepen our connection, our romance and our union. When many of you call on me at the same time, I expand as much as needed, so that I can personally be there for each of you simultaneously.

All the universes, galaxies, solar systems, stars and planets were created for one purpose: for you to explore your potential, expand your capabilities and evolve in unimaginable ways; for you to enjoy and experience everything that your heart desires.

Through all of your adventures, it is my hope that one day you will wonder about the purpose of life, the true nature of your being and the source of all existence. One day you will look beyond your worldly playthings and playmates, your stories and plans, your wounding and accomplishments. One day you will seek to go beyond the illusion and find the eternal reality. One day you will be ready to behold the magnificence, the beauty, the power of your soul and God. One day you will discover that the ultimate purpose of creation is love - love for yourself, love for each other, love for nature and love for God.

Journal

CHAPTER 40

Thousands of Christs, Krishnas & Buddhas

Rohit: Where do we go from here? What does the future hold for humanity?

God: There has never been a time like this. A remarkable era has begun for humankind all over the world. During the past century, every aspect of human life underwent monumental change. Society, politics, religion, technology and every aspect of human life changed in ways that could never have been imagined. This unbridled change was accompanied by massive environmental damage and large scale, violent upheavals. As the darkness grew, so too did the light. Thousands of highly evolved beings from across the Universe were born as humans and began teaching, coaching and guiding people to raise their consciousness. Millions of people, throughout the world, awakened spiritually, raising the vibrational energy of the planet. This massive spiritual resurgence resulted in a critical mass of high frequency energy that is healing the planet. In time, it is hoped that humans will see the light and welcome in a new era of peace, harmony and abundance for all on planet Earth. If they don't, then humanity will become extinct and replaced by a more evolved species capable of sustainable, harmonious living and spiritual growth.

The time has come for thousands of Christs, Krishnas, Buddhas and free souls to inundate the world with this message of hope, peace and love. They are here now, serving humanity, freeing people from the slavery of fear based thinking that has plagued this planet for centuries. There is no need to follow any of them. They are not saviors, messiahs or gurus. They do not have any magic formulas that will save the world. They are here to show you how to silence your mind so that you may follow your heart and discover your soul.

Do you remember the song 'Imagine' by John Lennon? It goes like this, "imagine there's no Heaven. It's easy if you try. No hell below us, above us only sky. Imagine all the people, living for today. Imagine there's no countries. It isn't hard to do. Nothing to kill or die for and no religion too. Imagine all the people living life in peace. Imagine no possessions, I wonder if you can. No need for greed or hunger, a brotherhood of man. Imagine all the people, sharing all the world." I inspired him to write that. I was sowing the seeds of change and reaching out with the same message that I am now sharing with you here. Imagine a world where God is the spirit of love and worshiping God means loving each other unconditionally, deeply, without judgment or discrimination. Imagine a world where no one is better than another, where everyone has an abundance of all that they need. Imagine a world without countries, borders, laws, discrimination, capitalistic exploitation, economic disparity, war, poverty, marriage, priests, judges or prisons. Imagine a world where everyone is free to live as they choose, where everything is shared, where there is no exploitation, no rich or poor, no bosses or owners, no rulers or governments. Imagine a world where there is freedom, peace and prosperity for everyone. In a world without taxes, financial institutions, banks, or stock markets, the only currency you will need are your services, creations or products and the only law you will need is a respect for everyone's free will. As long as people are compassionate, respectful, loving and honor one another's free will, they can never harm each other. This is not some idyllic pie in the sky fantasy. Such societies exist all across the Universe and have existed on planet Earth as well. If you want more details call me. I will gladly speak with you and show you how this can be achieved.

If you find it hard to believe what I am saying please consider that what you have seen, heard, read, thought and experienced up until now might be blocking you from imagining another possibility. You may have been brainwashed by the beliefs and ideologies that have been the cause of all the conflict, war, murder, greed, chaos and exploitation that you see all around you. Unless you change the way you think, unless you are willing to dream a better dream, unless you dare to step out of the box that you live in, things will go from bad to worse. In the heart and soul of every human being, there lies a dream of a paradise where you and your descendants can live in peace and harmony. Within each of you lies the blueprint for a better world that you all deserve.

Through books like this one and others, I am reaching out to all of you to create a tidal wave of inner change. I have been flooding the planet with messages that are not shrouded in the mystery and ambiguity of ancient languages but are easy to understand and follow. I have decided to become media savvy and flood the Earth with my words, using all the media available at your disposal like books, internet, television, radio, cinema, music and art. All my messages speak of the same essence, although the details may differ according to the culture, understanding, evolution and the transparency of the person I speak through.

It is not that I am perfect or have all the answers. Only you know what is true for you and what will work best for you. Do not blindly believe what I say, do not follow anyone, do not join any institution and most importantly, do not give away your free will or your power, for in doing so you will become weak and arrest your spiritual growth. Do not believe anything other than your inner voice. Learn to connect with your soul, listen to its soulful whispers inspiring and guiding you. What you hear from within will be perfectly true for you and will help you understand yourself as no one can and ever will. When you act on this inner guidance you will see yourself, the world and the Universe in a completely different light.

You are all brilliant, special, gifted and powerful souls. Each of you has special qualities and talents that make you extraordinary in unique ways. No one is better than anyone, no one has been chosen over anyone, no one is more or less dear to me. We need everyone's help. All of you have been chosen. Your primary task is to save yourself by uplifting your consciousness and, in doing so, you'll uplift the consciousness of this planet. That is the most powerful way to save the world and yourselves. Join hands, unite and collaborate for God's sake, for your sake, for the sake of your children and this beautiful planet. Learn to love, respect and value each other. Learn to be happy, content and peaceful in all circumstances.

Rohit: If thousands of Christs, Krishnas and Buddhas walk the Earth, will they not produce more religions and add to our problems? Nothing will change. The outcome will be the same as we have seen.

God: What you allude to is a fear filled scenario. Try looking at it from a different perspective. Life, through all its twists and turns, trials and tribulations, is designed to ultimately bring you back to yourself and God. You cannot go astray. No matter which way the road winds, it will always bring you back home. No matter which religion, guru or ideology they follow, eventually every truth seeker will, at some point in their journey, put aside everything that they know, turn within and seek me out. It matters little if one starts out as a Christian, Jew, Muslim, Hindu, Sikh or the follower of any other religion or sect. The truth is that any attempt to reach me, through any means, is always the right one and every path ultimately leads to me.

Rohit: You said there was an urgency and that we must act quickly! How can another round of messiahs and messengers possibly help us?

God: There is an urgency and there is not. If this planet weren't in serious danger I wouldn't bother. It makes no difference if you destroy this planet or blow yourselves up into smithereens. Energy is never destroyed. Everything will manifest again and everyone will recreate themselves. From my perspective, it's all child's play. In the words of Shakespeare, "it is a tale told by an idiot, full of sound and fury, signifying nothing." Yet I have been asked to intervene, to speak for the millions of souls across the Universe who care for you and love this planet. They feel that you will hear my words, that I may be able to wake you up and get you to take action. That's why I am here, at your service.

By increasing the number of teachers we are only increasing the diversity, the curiosity and the awareness. This time around the message is very clear. Discover yourself, understand God and love each other. Focus on inner peace and a direct connection with God. Once this connection is established it will always be there. It will gradually become the foundation of your life. As you start to trust your inner voice your spiritual growth will progress rapidly. You will begin to align yourself with your soul's nature. Your life will begin to flow effortlessly and miraculously. Your so called challenges will no longer disturb you. You will easily learn life's lessons, your progress will be quick, your growth accelerated and your transformation astounding.

Journal

CHAPTER 41

Eclectic Wisdom

Rohit: Are you implying that we should reject all religions and scriptures, that we should not go to Temples, Churches, Gurdwaras, Mosques and Synagogues?

God: Certainly not! Go everywhere! Do not limit or exclude me from any place. Wherever anyone remembers God is a sacred place. All scriptures are books about God and in all of them you will find some truth about me. All followers are your brothers and sisters, fellow travelers on a similar journey. Join them in their worship without judging, discouraging or criticizing them. Everyone is following the path that is perfect for them and no one is better or worse, right or wrong. Those who follow a particular religion, sect or path are often closed to all others. They will try to shut you out with clever arguments. Do not argue or try to prove anything. Respect and honor everyone. Embedded within every teaching are fragments of truth that in time will bring them closer to me.

Wherever you go, share your loving heart, your free spirit, your infinite peace. Be caring, empathetic and present. Do not be attached to any belief or ideology including what I am telling you here. There is wisdom and beauty in everyone waiting to reveal itself, longing to be witnessed by you.

When you live from your heart, your energy will be powerful and your thinking clear. People will seek you out. Share of your self with love and compassion, without argument, defensiveness or righteousness. Join in, sing, dance and pray with them. Your way is no more correct than their way. To even think that you are better is a product of the diseased ego. There is no better way! Every way is the right way. Every path leads to me. Every scripture and its preacher glorifies only me.

I am everywhere. Wherever you go, I am with you, always. Look for me and you will find me in everything and everyone. Recognize me in the eyes, the expressions and actions of those whom you meet. Hear me in the words they speak. Notice my little, everyday miracles in your life. I come to you in the most unexpected places and through the most unlikely people. A child, a stranger or a song may say something that could change your life forever. The world is full of your guides and teachers, whether they are aware of it or not. I speak to you through them. I make them say what you need to hear.

The ultimate litmus test for any spiritual teaching is this: if it makes you feel guilty or fearful; if it judges, discriminates or punishes in anyway; if it tells you how to live your life, moralizes, ties you down with rules and rituals; if it takes away your opinions, your free will or your individuality; if it separates you from others, tells you that you are better than them or produces disunity and hatred, then know for certain that this teaching has been misinterpreted and distorted. In which case, take from them that which will support, illuminate and inspire you on your journey.

Leave the rest and move on.

To quote Shakespeare once again, "a fool thinks himself to be wise, but a wise man knows himself to be a fool." Be a fool and you will keep learning. One who thinks he has the answers will stagnate and become obsolete. Children know nothing, they are happy and spread happiness. Fanatics think they know everything, they are miserable and spread misery everywhere. Your challenge is to find wisdom wherever you go. Knowledge is static and finite. Wisdom is dynamic and unending. Be an eclectic, listen, observe, explore, remain curious and you will find inspiration in the most unlikely places. New insights and realizations can come through anyone, anywhere. A single word, an idea or experience can open doors into unimaginable realms. The light of wisdom will dispel darkness, chaos, fear and doubt. It will uplift you and show the way.

Life is your greatest teacher and the whispers of your soul are your personal scripture, savior and guru. Life lessons learnt by trial and error, by mind generated ideas and strategies are likely to be filled with pain and suffering. Listening to your inner voice will ease your path. Situations will certainly arise but you will find yourself navigating them with ease and grace.

Record your experiences, your realizations, your wisdom and your struggles to live soulfully. Share your journey, your process, your discoveries and the challenges you faced. The more vulnerable and transparent you are, the more your life will inspire others.

Journal

CHAPTER 42

Loving God Fearlessly

Rohit: What message do you have for those who are already part of some religion, spiritual group or sect?

God: Whatever path you are on is the right path for you. It is a place where you have found solace, peace and some understanding of God but at the same time, know that the scripture you follow is neither holy, sacred nor is it the word of God. The savior, messiah or messenger is not God. He is a sincere lover of God and is very dear to me. He is not by any means perfect, pure or flawless. Belittling other faiths or fighting in his name will not endear you to me. He came for a purpose and that work is done. It is time to move to the next level of consciousness. To truly follow him please walk in his footsteps, to do as he did and be as he was.

Be your own unique version of Christ, Buddha, Krishna, Mohammed or any of the great souls that walked this earth. They did not follow any scripture, they did not go to a church, temple, mosque or synagogue. They listened to their inner voice, the voice of God, speaking to them from within.

Broaden your vision and open your heart. You will see that everyone is my loved one and they are all here to guide and support you on your path to God. Stay with the positive teachings of the religion or path you are on. Rid yourself of all the rules and restrictions, the do's and don'ts, rights and wrongs. Disregard the fear-based threats of judgment, punishment and hell, because fear and love do not go well together and where there is fear you will never find God. The God you fear does not exist. The true God is one who loves everyone equally and unconditionally.

In the eyes of God, whatever you do is perfect, you are perfect as you are and you can do no wrong!

Theologians, preachers and gurus have spent their lives speculating and arguing about the nature of God. They have dissected the scriptures looking for hidden meanings, translating, interpreting and distorting them to suit their theories. Their attempts remind me of the fable of the blind men and an elephant that goes like this:

Once, a group of blind men came across an elephant. One grabbed its legs and proclaimed that the elephant resembled a tree, another touched its trunk and thought that it was like a snake and yet another touched its tail and thought it was a broom. In much the same way, religious leaders have fought over their limited realizations about God and argued with each other over the ages, each believing that their theories were the ultimate truth.

I beg you, please let go of your egos, your version of the truth, your scriptures and your religion. Stop trying to prove yourself right. As long as you try to prove your point you can never be right. Instead of words, allow the fragrance of your inner peace and the sweetness of your loving heart light the path to God. Your distorted theories have set religion against religion, man against man and nation against nation. I plead with each one of you to stop fighting, arguing and nitpicking. Let go of your differences and teach people how to love each other and God. Live together and with me in harmony and Oneness.

Journal

CHAPTER 43

Save Yourself Soulfully

Rohit: It seems to be a daunting and seemingly impossible task. How can we possibly make a difference?

God: Fear has been a cruel master that has forced you to struggle for survival. Fear has cut you off from your soul and God. It has filled your life with stress and anxiety. It has made you sad, lonely and powerless. Fear, guilt, punishment, judgment and righteousness are all the opposite of love. Any teaching, law or code of morality based on these can never be from God. I am Love. Only where there is uplifting, unconditional, unmotivated, unlimited, free and eternal love will you find God. Wherever love is tainted with fear, conditions, restrictions, rules, expectations and needs, know that the egoic mind has created devious ways to control and exploit. It is that simple!

Doomsday prophecies, visions of hell, fears of damnation are all child's play. Children scared of the dark and scaring each other! People afraid of their own mortality their shadows and the judgment of their own minds.

Dark is as natural as light. Hell and heaven, devil and God, good and evil, are not to be feared. They are the result of your disconnectedness from your soul and God.

Fear can never be the basis of lasting change, it will not transform people's attitudes, nor will it ever save the world. Fear is an illusion that will only disempower you. It will never lead you to your soul or God. Darkness will never manifest light. Any teaching that says that the believers are saved and the non believers are damned, can never be from God. I love everyone no matter whether they accept me, believe in me or do as I say. I have no commandments and no laws. I love you no matter what you do, think or believe. It doesn't matter if you love me or hate me, use me or abuse me, I know that all roads lead to me. Sooner or later you will discover the truth and we will be reunited.

The chaos all around is just as it was meant to be. No one needs to save the world. The planet will take care of it itself, the environment will heal, the Earth will purge all unwanted activity and balance itself, at any cost. No one needs to save your soul for it never did any wrong. You will never be judged or punished. You have all been doing exactly what you came here to do. You are perfect as you are. The world is perfect as it is.

If you want to save someone and make a difference in any way, free yourself from your fears, illusions, beliefs, theories, morals, religions, science, laws and governments. Do not waste your time blaming, judging or condemning anyone. Instead, take complete responsibility for your experience, your life and your journey.

The problems with the world lie within each of you, as do the solutions. The world does not exist except as a product of your mind and senses. The world is in you and you are the creator of the world you live in. No two people live in the same world. Everyone lives in their own version, interpretation or perception of the world.

To go to heaven you need only free yourself from the negativity of your judgmental, chattering and out of control mind. Once you do that, you will experience beauty, harmony and perfection all around and will begin to see the world as it is. With a silent mind you will discover the beauty of your inner being and your soul. When in its presence, you will find everything that you ever desired.

I have no favorites. You are all powerful and amazing beings. You are all wise, beautiful and evolved souls. You are all my sons and daughters. You are all my messengers. You are all here to raise the consciousness of the Universe. You are all particles of God, just as perfect, powerful, wise and beautiful as God.

Enlightenment is not something you will attain, it is who you are. If you want to see God, first see yourself. If you want to save the world first save yourself.

Until we meet again,
With all my love,
God.

Journal

About the Author

Rohit Juneja was born in New Delhi, grew up in Mumbai, India. He currently lives in San Diego, where he works as a Spiritual Director, Counselor and Life Coach for people all over the world. His life affirming insights, practical wisdom and heart based healing therapies have endeared him to people. He is considered by many to be a spiritual innovator and a thought leader.

His lifelong search for meaning led him to explore psychology, religion and mysticism. In Vrindavan, India, under the guidance of a devotional mystic, he learned to connect with Source and listen to the immense wisdom of his inner voice. This awakening led to prolific writing through which he received succinct answers that transformed his life.

To know more about Rohit you may go to his website www.rohitjuneja.com He also has a dedicated Facebook Author page at www.facebook.com/rohit.juneja.author

www.ingramcontent.com/pod-product-compliance
Lightning Source LLC
LaVergne TN
LVHW041606070426
835507LV00008B/164